T0077927

BECOMING
AEON

ADVENTURES IN POLITICAL AND
MYSTICAL PHILOSOPHY

JOHN EDGCOMB

authorHOUSE®

AuthorHouse™
1663 Liberty Drive
Bloomington, IN 47403
www.authorhouse.com
Phone: 833-262-8899

© 2020 John Edgcomb. All rights reserved.

No part of this book may be reproduced, stored in a retrieval system, or transmitted by any means without the written permission of the author.

Published by AuthorHouse   01/20/2021

ISBN: 978-1-7283-5827-7 (sc)
ISBN: 978-1-7283-5826-0 (e)

Print information available on the last page.

Any people depicted in stock imagery provided by Getty Images are models, and such images are being used for illustrative purposes only. Certain stock imagery © Getty Images.

This book is printed on acid-free paper.

Because of the dynamic nature of the Internet, any web addresses or links contained in this book may have changed since publication and may no longer be valid. The views expressed in this work are solely those of the author and do not necessarily reflect the views of the publisher, and the publisher hereby disclaims any responsibility for them.

Contents

The Aeons were intelligences and attributes of the Supreme God in ancient Gnostic philosophy, such as beauty, love, justice, and wisdom. I hope to come to you as an Aeon. Enlightening through this book. Describing many philosophical subjects to arrive at truth and wisdom.

Politics and Economics

Politics, the state, and politicians should promote Virtue, Moderation, Liberty(freedom to do what one wants as long as one is not harming others nor their property), Justice which is fairness and getting what one deserves, and be practical.

A great state and economy are conducive to contributing to individual liberty and thus to the attainment of mystical experience. When money is saved by the state the economy prospers if money is used frugally and prudently. When a lot of debt accumulates the economy degenerates because there is no money to provide for prosperity unless there are large amounts of resources and production to support the debt.

If someone does not want to participate in mutual self interest in the state then the person may voluntarily leave the state and live on one's own. Wise leaders will be determined by the characteristics of the wise man. In a great state people will be free to pursue their own self development and self exploration which is conducive to spiritual development. Some people will do this despite what the state is like but a well ordered state will make it easier for people to pursue. The best state is the best aid to mystical experience. People must learn on their own what is good for them. If the state bans what is not good for people the people will do what is bad for themselves anyway resisting the enforcement of the state. People have to realize what is good for themselves through their own experience.

Following are some rules in a state which maximizes individual freedom. Birth control and abortion will be permitted. Overpopulation and the deficiency of natural resources to maintain that population is an issue that will be addressed either through human regulation or by the limits of natural resources. The extremity of the situation will determine the extent of such regulations. The limits of natural resources will determine the size of the population. Pornography and prostitution will be permitted but all prostitutes and their clients must take a sexually transmitted disease test every time just before sexual intercourse and if they have an STD they will no longer be allowed to engage in sexual intercourse unless they use protection from STDs. Homosexuality and homosexual marriage will be permitted. The environment will be preserved. All drugs will be legal. This political system maximizes as much liberty as possible without allowing an individual to harm another individual, an individual's property, nor harm the environment. Maximizing liberty and minimizing harm is conducive to spiritual development. Being told the truth is not the same as living according to the truth. People must realize on their own the spiritual experience and what the truth is often through experience which is why they should have as much individual liberty as possible without harming others and without interfering with the individual liberty of others.

The utilitarian theme that what is good for the greatest number is good is a tautology. It is true by definition. Utilitarianism is true stating that what benefits the most people is good. What is good for the greatest number of people is the perfection of the people and to bring them closer to their purpose, the realization of their essence which is the spiritual experience through living a good life. Most people must realize this by themselves which makes individual liberty essential as people must explore in their own ways to come to the truth. People should be allowed to do whatever they want as long as they are not harming anyone else and anyone else's property. People should do what they want even if doing what they want harms them as long as they are not harming anyone else and things that anyone else are using. Mill was right when he thought that a person should be allowed to do whatever he or she wants and have as much individual liberty as they want as long as he or she does not interfere with the individual liberty of other people and as long as they are not harming things that belong to other people. Many mystics have developed themselves by following their own way of individual liberty, self sufficiency, and independence.

Judging from history there will never be an ideal state. The world will never change, it will always remain as wicked and as good as it is. Throughout history there has always been war, poverty, and suffering. The imperfections of the government and community will stay the way they are. The individual has very limited power in influencing the conditions of the world. But one may be good and thus make the world better by being good one's self. We must not try to conquer or change the world because conquering or changing the world is not in any one person's control. Instead of changing the world, the individual must overcome himself or herself which is realized in wisdom.

If a wise man was able to rule a state he could still not make the people of that state be wise. At most he could try to convince them to be good and wise. According to history it is impossible to create an ideal state as there never has been a successful one. The best political philosophy proposed is Plato's. The only thing that is wrong with it is that the philosopher kings cannot stop the unenlightened people from revolting and establishing a tyrannical regime. The only thing would be a police force in which the philosopher kings have complete control over to do justice. Even if the philosopher kings had this police force under their control the masses could still revolt and establish a tyrannical regime. A state is good if its people are good. If the people of a state are vulgar, the state will be vulgar. This means that it is highly unlikely that there will ever be an ideal state because it is impossible for one person to make another person do what should be done. It is impossible for a good person to make a person who is not persuaded by what is good to be good. At best the good person could convince the person who is not good to be good. A good state will have virtuous and good inhabitants. A bad state will have bad inhabitants. The more good inhabitants a state has the better the state will be and no one can make a person be good except the person himself or herself. If the person chooses to be a good person then the state will be better because it has a good inhabitant. The characteristics of the wise man are good characteristics which inhabitants of a state must have in order for the state to be a good state. Since no one can make people be good but can only convince them to be good and people are usually not convinced by others to be good, it is highly unlikely that the ideal state will ever happen. A state is good only in so far as its inhabitants are good. It is possible that an ideal state will happen but it is highly unlikely. The state will change when the people change.

Social and Economic Coercion

Justice is fairness and getting what one deserves. People present themselves using technology and get paid large amounts of money to talk about nonsense while those who work in essential services such as janitors and garbage men get paid very little. People go into politics to make money at the expense of those they are supposed to represent. There are constant wars which are encouraged by the military industrial congressional complex and the arms trade in which large amounts of money are made selling weapons to those fighting the wars. One should use such activities to one's advantage for the good.

People in society are coerced and coerce others to conform and become something they would rather not be. People are coerced to look for work and work in jobs they do not want in order to survive and preserve their physical existence. People are coerced in society to conform and work in jobs that are unethical in order to have basic material possessions in society. Society is indirectly telling people to either conform and work, or become houseless and have a painful and desperate life. Through this coercion people are made to conform and not be true to themselves in society. For example one may not want to be a factory worker but the only jobs which are available are factory jobs and in order to avoid poverty a person must take a factory job and be a factory worker. People are wage slaves in that they work for very little. They have the choice to quit their job but if they do they will become very poor. People get paid small amounts of money to do a lot of work while some people get paid large amounts of money and do barely any work at all. The economic demand leads people to take jobs they don't really want but have to take to be a part of society and keep up with the economic standard of living. People pursue employment in positions they do not want but do so because the economy and the system coerce and encourage them to do so. This means of coercion is alienating and dehumanizing especially when a person is paid very little for one's labor. One should be what one wants to be and should not be hindered by economic and social demands placed on the individual. Many compulsions and coercions of society such as schools have been against an individual's freedom of spirit, therefore you should not do what society wants you to do. As Marcus Aurelius said one's life is very short, so you should only conform to your nature, know yourself, be yourself.

There are many useful things existing in society which encourage individuals to conform. Technology, media, improvements in healthcare and the quality of food, and conformity by most people encourage individuals to conform. What an individual wants to do as a career is often unavailable in society which means an individual has a better chance of being employed if he or she accepts a position which he or she does not want but is available. Therefore the more an individual conforms to society and is willing to take whatever is available, the greater chance an individual will have economic security in society. This is a subtle form of social and economic coercion. Individuals are encouraged to conform and be someone they are not.

The maxim that capitalism turns luxuries into necessities is true. At one time cars were considered luxuries, now they are necessities as cities are spread so far apart with inconvenient and inefficient public transportation that one must have an automobile to function in society. Computers were once unnecessary luxuries, now computers are used for everything in society and one must have a computer in order to function in society.

In a class system people are alienated from one another. In a system where everyone pursues their own selfish interests people are alienated from one another and no real community or fellowship is possible. A syncretism of socialism and capitalism is best.

Technology and entertainment through technology are used to distract people from what's important. For example Sports and entertainment distract people from political and economic issues which effect their lives. Entertainment and technology distract people from the oppression they undergo by the political system. One views so many images when one watches television that one is distracted from more important issues. Technology is used to coerce people to conform. Technology is used to control and manipulate people to conform to the system. Technology deludes people about what is true in the world and in reality. The advancement of technology is inevitable and therefore people must learn to control technology so technology does not control their lives.

When people use electrical technology they expose their bodies to electricity which heats the body and may irritate their mental condition to a small extent. However technology such as television is used to relieve frustration and anxiety. Although if so much frustration and anxiety was not caused by technology such as the noise from cars, people would not need technology to relieve the frustration which the technology causes.

Technology is used to spy on people which has terrible consequences for the future of society. Privacy is not respected. People are too petty, selfish, and unintelligent to solve the problem which will either cease by force, collapse, or disintegrate and move on to something else such as another problem or another way of life.

Technology is a very resourceful, convenient, entertaining, and useful tool. It is one of the crowning achievements of the human race. But it should be acknowledged that it is used to present many deceitful appearances and is used in many deceitful ways. And one should control the technology and use it to the benefit of one's self. One should not have one's self controlled and used for the benefit of Technology.

The luxuries of society are used to coerce people to conform to the system. If one wants to be free from one's job and the system one may do so but society uses luxuries such as tools and items for cleaning teeth, food, shelter, and tremendous conformity to discourage people from choosing to be houseless and live a much more free and less bonded life. Without money one could not buy items to keep one's teeth clean which may result in cavities, toothache, and severe pain. Possibilities like these discourage people from leaving their jobs and places in society and live a much more free and happier life. The more these luxuries develop and improve, the more specialized the labor becomes in order to make these luxuries, the more dependent people become on other people in society to maintain this standard of living, the more people will be bonded to the system and their place in society. Thus the more difficult it will be for people to overcome these fears and give up their job and material possessions as well as truly pursue what they want to do in their lives. Most people are slaves to the economy and the system. The Promotion of Economic Growth is used to make people conform and support the system. The more technology advances the more people are dependent on the system.

Today civilization is too specialized. It takes years to get the requirements people have to have in order to get a particular job even though they can do the job without the requirements. People are conditioned into a certain way of thinking based on their specialty. Overspecialization and over organization are dangerous aspects of technological society in terms of restricting and limiting the creativity and freedom of individuals. When one is taught to think in one particular way it discourages other ways of thinking. When people are coerced and intimidated by threats of poverty and social rejection, they are encouraged to conform to be something other than themselves which they usually do not want to be. It is necessary to limit the freedom to harm others in society and to interfere with the convenience of other people's lives, but the freedom to be creative individuals should not be discouraged nor restricted. And freedom of individual creativity is restricted and discouraged through overspecialization, over organization, and conformity.

In some places people value economic growth which is not necessarily a good thing. Economic growth induces more technology, specialization, and alienation. Sometimes people encourage economic growth because they are poor and exploited by the system which overworks and underpays them. People would not be so enthusiastic of economic growth if most of the wealth was not possessed by only a few people compared to most of the population. People would not be so enthusiastic about economic growth if wealth disparity was not so high. Economic growth promotes materialism over spiritual aspects of life. The encouragement of economic growth and having a good economy is used to invade and oppress other peoples and cultures who are considered poor. They are considered to have a bad economy compared to industrialized economies. Those industrialized economies claim that non industrialized economies are poor economies and bad. Those who do not have the same cultures, industry, and economy as industrialized economies are considered inferior and in a poor condition. Economic growth is used to make people conform and support the current system. The happiest countries in the world are not those which seek to maximize gross domestic product, but those which are most spiritually fulfilled.

Political Problems

I am writing concerning recent legislation regarding public money being spent for private school expenditures. Regarding religious schools the legislation is clearly unconstitutional. Most of the people who applied for the subsidy are of a higher than average income demographic and would send their children to private schools anyway. The state should not subsidize wealthy people who do not need the money. When governments fund private institutions they gain more power over those institutions as a result of giving them money. This will make private institutions more likely to adhere to government policy when not adhering to such policy may result in ceasing to be given government funds. The private institutions will most likely adhere to government policy when their government funding is threatened. People who do not want to send their children to state and taxpayer funded schools should not be subsidized for sending their children to a private school while they have the option of attending public school.

There should be a progressive state income tax in which income tax is determined by how much an individual makes. The more one makes, the higher a percentage of their income should be taxed. Wealth inequality in the U.S.A. is higher than in any other industrialized nation. People who make the most money often do not make the most beneficial contribution to society such as investment bankers. And those who make much less make a much more beneficial contribution such as garbage men and janitors.

Insurance premiums are too high. Insurance companies only care about making money and do everything they can to deny coverage and payments to their clients. Because of this they will not provide coverage and will only seek to make money. People who need Healthcare immediately will not be able to check to see if they are covered. They should not have to check to see if their health insurance covers their medical bills before they get healthcare.

Automobiles: There are too many automobiles, they are a huge waste of nonrenewable resources. They are extremely dangerous. They should not have built the country to be so dependent on them and should build the country to be less dependent on them and be more dependent on trains. They are noisy, expensive, and bad for the environment.

Sports: Sports players and the people involved in sports make too much money with no good contribution to society. They should not make so much money. Sports events should be taxed so they can have a productive contribution to the economy.

Football stadium: The Raiders football stadium attempting to be built in Las Vegas should not be subsidized by the government. Billionaires should not receive government subsidies, especially for football stadiums.

Government spending: The government wastes much of the money they spend and should spend it more efficiently.

Wealth Inequality

There is too much wealth inequality. The wealthiest people have too much while the poorest have too little. Laws should be implemented enforcing a more equal distribution of wealth in which people are not allowed to make so much more than their employees.

There is a tendency of Americans to ignore the wealth inequality which exists around them. They tend to just get on in their lives and ignore the fact that some of their fellow citizens make a tremendous amount of money more than they do while they either make much less or are struggling to survive. They are kept under control by their fear, laziness, and lack of confidence as well as the system which oppresses them.

School Institutions

The school system is inefficient and not worth doing. I may do something to improve the current condition of schooling as a teacher operating within the school system. However most people will not change therefore the school system and the state will not change. Change can come gradually with reform movements which never accomplish what they intend to achieve but nevertheless gradually improve conditions to a small extent. The Universities hinder the student's pursuit of truth rather than guiding them to the truth. One would acquire a better education if one did not attend the Universities and State schools rather than if one did. The Universities and State schools are a waste of time and money. Of course some schooling and education is better than no schooling nor education. The teachers make the subject so uninteresting that the students are uninterested. Students are not interested in the subjects the schools teach to begin with. They do not care about the subject and just attend school because they are required by the law to attend school. The assignments which the teachers assign do not encourage learning. They add to the student's load of busy work. Most of the time in public schools is wasted and is not educational. The way the current system of learning is set up in which students are talked at by the teachers all day is highly uneducational. The teachers say many superfluous things about their subject while they could discuss things which would increase the efficiency of the purpose which is learning.

Most people enroll in Universities in order to get a degree so that they can get a high paying job. This is not a good reason to attend a University. The goal of a University education is to acquire an education in order to lead a better life. The University requirements have become a bureaucracy in which the student must fulfill the requirements and concentrate on fulfilling the requirements of the University rather than on gaining an education. The student must concentrate on getting good grades and so do the work according to how the "teacher" wants the work to be done rather than how it should be done so as the student learns something. This further hinders the student from learning. Grades and mandatory attendance should be abolished so that learning would be much easier. The courses which the student takes are so specialized and so little material is covered in them that the student loses interest. There are many distractions in the classroom such as noise which distract the students from paying attention to the lecture.

One may acquire a good education on the computer. The only thing a computer does not offer is discussion with another person. Often those at the University including professors are not worth discussing with. University professors are overpaid and under worked and have cushy jobs. Most of them should not get the privileges they get. Many people who have PhDs are not good teachers and are uneducated themselves. Massive funds are given to schools and research programs which will not gain many benefits and are wasted. Much money is spent on the state education system and often after many years the people who go through the system are uneducated. Schools should be oriented towards learning and there should be no financial incentive for attending schools. Otherwise people will only attend schools for financial gain. People may learn on their own with libraries and computers. Universities may be places of learning and discussion.

Currently in the era of specialization everyone is a specialist and cannot acquire a job without the degree in that specific field. Many times one who does not have a degree in a certain subject could do the job better than one who does have a degree in the subject. People with the skills necessary to do a certain job cannot get the job because they do not have the degree or piece of paper which a person wants to see to get the job. While others have a degree and get the job even though their skills are inferior to those who have the skills but do not have the degree. Most people go to college not to acquire an education but to get a degree so they can get a high paying job. These requirements of a degree with no real skills should be abolished so that people who know how to do the job well may get the job whether or not they have a degree. Their skills may be confirmed through demonstrations.

The state of the educational institutions is not new. They are more accurately called the institutions of social oppression. Schopenhauer, Nietzsche, Russell Kirk, and Noam Chomsky all write of the horrible condition of the educational system. Rousseau also writes that colleges do not educate people.

The schools may have represented good intentions but they are used to encourage stupidity and conformity. Most institutions present an appearance of doing good but in fact they do little good or do the opposite of what they claim to be doing. The government, healthcare, education, the military, and societal systems are wasteful and inefficient. People get jobs and positions based on luck, chance, and connections to other people. This is a problem of intrinsic human corruption rather than a problem of any social or economic system such as capitalism or socialism. Universities and schools do more to conceal the truth than they do to reveal the truth.

University Expansion

The universities are businesses seeking to expand their wealth and power as much as possible. They constantly try to build new buildings, gain more money, and increase enrollments at the expense of the quality of education. Students do not attend universities to learn but to attain a high income job. The universities do a lousy job teaching as they are inefficient and waste time and money. Universities will teach only one doctrine of liberalism and ignore other philosophies. Faculty will hire only liberals who conform to their views and the bureaucracy.

The universities lower standards in order to increase enrollments and accumulate money to expand.

Universities are preoccupied with sociability and cater demands to increase vocational training at the expense of education. Universities promote mediocrity, intellectual irrelevance and waste time, no one needs four years in a university, much less 13 years in public school to be educated. They promote moral relativism which defeats the purpose of education. The students do not want to be educated, most are uneducable. The students become bored and resentful with the lousy system they are told to attend for their own good and only cooperate with the false promise of getting a job that will make them more money. Most students do not attain the wealth or career the University promises.

Universities should be defunded and become smaller. Establish separate trade schools for students with the sole interest of making money, and limit the university courses to the humanities and sciences. Those whose incentive is to learn and not make money will be attracted to a university and possibly acquire a liberal education. Universities are a reflection of the larger society. And the society of the United States is extremely in favor of business, the pursuit of wealth no matter the costs, and cultural relativism. There is only one party in the United States, the business party.

Education

Education has so much to do with memory. If one cannot remember what one has learned, then one has not learned and cannot utilize and recall the things that will improve one's life. If one has forgotten one's education it is as though one never attained an education. If one has forgotten an aspect of one's education then one can no longer use the aspect of one's education to improve one's life or retain a good quality of living. Education also has much to do with discipline. Only one who has discipline and can sustain and persevere in one's discipline is intelligent or has acquired one's discipline in education. Education has much to do with having the discipline to do what's right. It has to do with the discipline to control and conquer one's lust. One must have the discipline to control one's passions and to take care of one's self. The educated person avoids anger.

One must be able to think for one's self and think critically to be educated. One must also have self control, discipline, and be able to remember what one has learned. One must have virtue in the forms of justice (fairness and being able to discern what people deserve), courage (for example to act justly when one is pressured not to), moderation, and wisdom (understanding fundamental concepts and principles of existence) which involves prudence, and thinking critically and thinking for one's self. Also one must have good manners, politeness, respect, and good propriety in order to be educated. One must have these things in order to be educated. There are degrees of education in that people who have some of these traits are more educated than people who have none of these traits. People who have these traits without having been educated by another person or external source possess the quality of intelligence.

Education is support for intuitive reason leading to the attainment and attaining of spiritual liberation. And that is the only education worthy of the name. Schooling is help towards education at most. And schooling cannot help those who are uneducable. We are educated to the degree and extent that we have intuitive reason and are spiritually liberated.

The end of a liberal education is death. The realization that the purpose of life is union with God which includes the end of this world in its futility and vanity. After union with God is attained nothing is left to do, and death follows, only being in God is perfect, and everything outside of God is imperfect, thus once perfection is attained, the end is achieved, and there is either regression back to life, or completion and the end in death. But in death the soul is in an eternity with the One.

Philosophy and other Subjects

In Philosophy, there is no distinction between art and science. All academic subjects are subjects of philosophy. Philosophy is the core. Specialization leaves people in continuous partial understanding. When we are concentrating on the whole we cannot concentrate on the parts and vice versa, thus when concentrating on the parts we cannot comprehend the whole, and the universal truth. One should know a little about all subjects and not just a lot about one subject in order to have a more complete understanding of existence. All speech and writing is just commentary on existence.

Aristotle wrote all human life is sunk deep in untruth. The world always drifts off into unreason. As Plato wrote the world is illusion. One must turn within oneself to find the reason following one's self. Following the world and other groups leads to unreason. Reason is the mind coming to understand the good and the universe.One must turn within oneself to find the Truth and the good. One should conduct one's life in moderation. Use one's mind for reason and use logic to come to correct conclusions. One should control one's appetites. This is the good life.Even today the life of Socrates, the life of the philosopher, is the good life and the best life amid all the advanced technology. One who lives the same as Socrates like a wise owl lives the wisest and best life.

Ethics

There is a very easy way to show that all statements are ethical statements in terms of their being true or false. A true statement is a good statement because it is true. A false or dishonest statement is bad because it is false and dishonest. For example the statement many things fall downwards towards the earth because of gravity is a true statement. To deny the truth of the statement would be bad. Since it is a true statement it must be a good statement because of its truth. Anyone who disagrees with me would think that there view is true and therefore a better view than my view. Since they think their view is better they would think my view is worse than their view. Since they think my view is worse they think their view is more good or better than my view. Therefore any true statement has goodness attached to it. Any false statement has badness attached to it. Good and bad are inherent in true and false statements. Therefore a true statement is a good statement. Since being good is part of morality a good statement is therefore a moral statement.

Sexual Desire

Sexual desire can only be overcome if one attains to higher metaphysical realities, or attains grace. Once one's state of mind has realized that having higher states of consciousness is better, happier, and more pleasurable than sex one has overcome sexual desire. Sexual desire is absurd in that one's sexual desire for another is completely determined by how that person or object looks. And just under the skin of the beautiful person is blood and flesh which is not as beautiful and sexual as the superficial beauty of the person. Therefore a beautiful body is an illusion and the body is subject to change which means a beautiful body one day may not be a beautiful body the next day. Sexual desire is very vane too. If we don't think a person's body is attractive, we will find another body for the object of our sexual desire. And once our sexual desires are attained, new desires take their place and we remain unsatisfied. Sex is pleasurable but has painful consequences. The body has to recover from sex. Among the negative consequences of sexual desire after masturbation and ejaculation are the energy depletion of the body, fatigue, hunger, feeling dirty, more often defecation and farting, feelings of gloominess and grogginess, increased hair and nail growth, more acne, hair feeling dirty, and sometimes eyes hurting.

In the long run sex is not pleasurable. Sexual desire is overcome and conquered by realizing that having a higher intellect and attaining a higher metaphysical state of consciousness is better, happier, and more pleasurable than the temporary fulfillment of sexual desire. We must attain that higher state to be enlightened and liberated.

Some positive aspects of the fulfillment of sexual desire through masturbation is it can relieve temporarily frustration, stress, and anxiety. It is very pleasurable for a short time. But then one would have unpleasurable experiences for a longer time.

To escape the negative consequence of masturbation and ejaculation previously written through death would not work. In doing so the person would feel sadness just before death in their expiration in which the body and mind would depreciate to death and it would not result in a pleasurable nor happy experience just before death.

In order to conquer sexual desire one must transcend nature and reach higher states of spiritual consciousness.

One must abandon sex to reach union with god, sex bonds us to life and the world which is why it is condemned by the religions. It is not evil and is a worldly pleasure. One just needs to abandon it to transcend the world and life to reach union with God. Sex is not as bad as the religions particularly Christianity claim it is.

On Being One's Self

One should strive to be one's self and be what one wants to be, no one knew this better than Emerson and Nietzsche. All great people, artists, philosophers, saints, and founders of great religions, are still subject to the bizarre streams of thought and temptations as everyone else. They still have bodies which defecate and carry out various bodily functions. But they have made something greater than these base things and have raised themselves to a better state. As long as one is alive one will be subject to base things. But great people transcend these base things through art and the intellect. As long as one is alive one will be attached to a body and be in the realm of mind. Mind is the realm of association of ideas and streams of consciousness. But great people go beyond mind and body while they are alive and participate in better things such as art and the intellect. These better things make life more valuable and interesting.

The great individuals of the past must have overcome doubt in themselves and all the economic hardships and obstacles to follow their hearts, pursue their art or writings and express their greatness. I have thought of many fears of danger and poverty which may involve being yourself and pursuing what one wants to do as opposed to what one must do to economically support one's self. An individual must overcome all their fears of poverty and economic obstacles and pursue their art or writing despite economic insecurities in order to become great. A person can survive and be happy on very little.

An individual must transcend the times he or she is born in to become great. We are born into a particular time with particular norms. Individuals must transcend the time and culture they are born into to grasp what is universally true and good for all times. All great individuals are universal. Their ideas are universally true and good.

The antithesis between the existential doctrine to be one's self and the religious doctrine to obey god and what is supremely good is solved in realizing that being one's self and obeying the supreme good is what one really should be striving for and are really the same thing. Not simply being one's self but being what one truly is and ought to be are the same thing. An authentic self is true to itself and one that is true to its essence. By following truth one is really true to one's self and discovers what one should be which is one's essence and is God.

On Nietzsche's Philosophy

In Twilight of the Idols Nietzsche writes of how the false world became the true world. He calls it the history of a lie. He implies that people stopped believing in the true world and objective truth.

In Medieval times people have found the true world, the true world is God, the true world is the kingdom of heaven within your mind, the false world is the Devil, our senses, and matter. The false world is a deception.

In the 19th century & 20th century people thought there is no true world! The true world is a lie, a fabrication, a world in flux contains no reality, there is no true world. Nietzsche was artistic and thought there is no reality nor objective truth.

Nietzsche's postmodernism and the legacy of Nietzsche is the idea that the individual must grow and develop into something great and overcome the burdens and obstacles which the herd places in front of the individual in order to cast the individual into doubt, confusion, and diffidence which prevent him from realizing his true potential and developing it into creativity, intelligence, and genius. We create our own truths which are our own forms of greatness unique unto themselves and constituting grandness and sublimity. By creating our own truths and forms of greatness we overcome the tyranny of modern industrial society which takes the form of conformity, pettiness, and normative views of what is good and evil.

Dionysus was the god of wine, that is, intoxication, that is, divine intoxication, that is, ecstasy. Nietzsche made Dionysus his god as the god of continuous change through sublimation moving from one experience of ecstasy to the next in continuous original creative self expression.

Critique of the History of Philosophy

The mainstream history of philosophy contains people who were chosen to be represented in its history. These people did not become famous solely out of their own merits although some of them are great philosophers. People were determined to be famous for future generations. There are many more thinkers who were at least as great as the famous philosophers who are much less well known. The history of Philosophy is set to include certain figures who were lucky enough to be picked to be part of that history. People alive today who are not good philosophers but are considered good philosophers today will be forgotten by future generations. These people get certain privileges while they are alive including professorships and attention. The history of philosophy includes these very small intellectual circles of people lucky enough to be part of them and thus is deficient and partial in this way. It is true that many great thinkers are not recognized during their life while other thinkers who are unintelligent and get professorships while they are alive are recognized during their life. Great thinkers who are not recognized during their time should leave something of their ideas behind whether in writing or in art. Some will recognize them for what they are.

The partiality of the history of Philosophy is true of other aspects of History. For example, the history of America is rather the history of European Settlement in America. History is written by the victor and the whole of U.S. history contains the history of Europeans and their posterity who settled in America. There is only a very small history of the natives who settled in America tens of thousands of years before the European settlers came. Western or European Philosophy dominates the history of Philosophy in the West which means the United States and Europe.

Philosophy of Mind

Philosophy begins in wonder. Perhaps philosophy begins with individualism. The issue of reductionism in philosophy has puzzled philosophers for a long time. It has been thought that the mind can be reduced to the atoms of the brain. Yet this theory is false. The mind or consciousness is not reducible to the atoms of the brain. We cannot fully comprehend the source of consciousness through such materialist reasoning. In order to understand what the mind is we must use intuition or intuitive reason. We contemplate within ourselves to understand that the mind is of an immaterial nature. All materialist explanations of the mind end with the question of how can matter induce mind and consciousness. What gives rise to consciousness is the thing which consciousness is dependent on or the cause of consciousness. Socrates said one should know thyself and According to the Alcibiades to know oneself is to know one's soul. The soul in ancient times meant the same thing as the mind means today. Of course a person could not have sense perception if one did not have the corresponding sense organs such as the eyes, ears, nose , and tongue; without these organs one could not see, hear, smell, or taste. Yet one must be conscious of one's senses in order to perceive them. And one could not have sense perception without consciousness. And the source and cause of consciousness has yet to be determined by science. This source and cause lies in the most profound part of the mind which can only be grasped intuitively and is beyond reason. Reason can only get us so far. Reason is the law of causality. It was a mistake of the enlightenment to presuppose that everything can be explained through reason. We must comprehend intuitively what the mind really is and what the source of the mind really is. This goes beyond reason. These methods of understanding the mind are unpopular in modern times. Yet when scientific inquiry is pushed to the limit in attempting to understand the mind researchers will pursue other methods to understand the mind.

Science

I will now consider the possibility of indivisible particles. These particles may be analogous to the atoms of Democritus and the monads of Leibniz. The indivisible particle must be dimensionless. If the particle contains any number of dimensions other than zero, then it is divisible. The question arises is there such a thing as dimensionless matter? When one cuts a piece of matter one can look closer at a piece of the cut matter and cut the matter again. This process would go on forever. Matter by definition contains dimensions and therefore will always be divisible. Therefore, the indivisible particle must not be material. The indivisible particle must be something like Leibniz's monad. If such spiritual substances exist, they would have to be dimensionless to be an indivisible particle. Suppose that physics finally reduces matter to one particle, suppose the particle is called a monad. The question would arise, what is this particle. The answer would most likely be pure energy. The question what is pure energy would arise. No matter how much scientists reduce matter to its most fundamental components the question will remain what is energy. Some think energy is electromagnetic waves. Electrons must exist for electricity and electromagnetic waves to exist and the question would arise what is an electron. Even if an electron was a bundle of pure energy the question would remain what is energy. The question would eventually arise why does electricity behave the way it does. The answer would be because opposite charges attract. The question arises why do they attract. Scientists do not explain why things are the way they are but explains how things are the way they are. Science does not explain what things are at their irreducible level. Scientists don't know ultimately why energy behaves the way it does but use the term to describe the phenomena they perceive. They manipulate energy but do not know why energy behaves the way it does. As all matter is reduced to pure energy, pure energy is simply what is or what has existence in philosophical terms. Energy is the spiritual love which all things are.

Art

The purpose of art is to attain higher states of feeling which include meaning and intrinsic value of what is truly beautiful through the senses. Art may express the way the world is at a given time or how someone feels about the world at a given time. These expressions of the artist may give a valid and true expression of the values, thoughts, and attitudes people have in the times they live in.

Many artists were Platonists. Among them were Michelangelo and Botticelli. Their art depicts various Platonic concepts. For example Botticelli 's Birth of Venus depicts a woman standing on a shell which is supposed to be the birth of the cosmos as an emanation from the shell. In various architecture and church art, pillars hold the walls of the churches and mosques and the ceiling is in the shape of a dome. The walls and the dome represent the various metaphysical hierarchies from intelligences to the Good, the One, and God, which are different names for the same thing.

The difference between noise and music is that noise is chaotic and music is harmonious. Music expresses harmony while noise brings sounds of chaos.

Vampires and Werewolves

The vampire is a metaphor for a person who has become completely evil. The vampire exists in eternal darkness. The vampire has eternal life in darkness or lives forever in darkness which is associated with the idea that the vampire can only come out at night. If the vampire comes out in the day time it is burned alive by the sun. The myth of the vampires vulnerability to the sun is that a person that is evil cannot see God which is associated with the sun and if he or she does see God (which is the supreme light) the evilness which is the vampires essence will be destroyed from exposure to God which the vampire being burned to death by the sun is an allegory for. The evil person being exposed to God will be defeated and destroyed.

The vampire sucks the blood of human beings. This is also a metaphor for an evil person taking the life energy of those who are not evil and making them evil. Blood is the life energy. A vampire sucks the blood of a human being and turns the human into a vampire. This is a metaphor for an evil person (the vampire) taking away the life energy of a person who is not evil by an evil action whether it be abuses and insults or physical harm and drives the person to become evil (to become a vampire). The vulnerability of the vampire to the cross and the death of the vampire through driving a wooden stake through the heart are also metaphors. The cross is a symbol of supreme goodness and the vampire being an evil creature is vulnerable to goodness. Likewise an evil person is vulnerable to goodness as good actions and people that are good. Like attracts like. Evil people do not like good people and try to hurt them to make good people more like them. Misery loves company. Regarding the myth that a vampire can be killed through a wooden stake through the heart. The heart is a symbol of love which the vampire or an evil person entirely lacks. By destroying a vampire heart which is the opposite of a good heart or a loving heart, (the vampires heart is a heart of evil) one destroys the vampire. Wood could be a symbol of life.The vampire can live in eternal darkness but must feed on the blood of the living. In order to remain a vampire in an evil state of being the vampire must continuously maintain its evil being by harming others.

It is said that one dies and goes to heaven. This is a metaphor for giving up one's self and one's particular personality to attain a universal self by embracing God which is a metaphor for dying and going to heaven. The person who becomes a vampire gives up his personality for an evil personality.

Were wolves represent people who let their sexual appetite control them. A werewolf can be killed by a silver bullet. In alchemy, silver represents the material mercury which is a symbol for wisdom. The were wolf can be defeated and destroyed by silver. That is, one's animal appetites can be overcome through wisdom.

Levels of Being

There are levels of being. Basically there are the levels of body, mind, and spirit. The level of the body is the level of the material world and one's own body which includes sensual stimulus. The level of mind is the level of one's mind which includes streams of consciousness, imagination, association of ideas, and thought. Levels of emotional, aesthetic, and moral thought and feeling are in between the realms of mind and spirit. The level of spirit is the level of intelligence, intellectual intuition, and God.

Neo Platonism

There is a hierarchy of being with the One at the top, Intelligences emanating from the One, the Soul and Mind, and Matter at the bottom. Reason, Virtue, together with discipline, control and effort and Intuition guide the soul to comprehension of the One. And all existence. The material world is a Theophany. All that exists is in the One, and the One is in all things. All in One, One in All. Determinism is true as human actions are determined. Existence is good. Matter is privation. The best life is to do and be the One. One may apprehend the One through many variations.

Theology

The experience of God is pleasurable, the supreme pleasure, I'm writing like a theologian.

Christians said the kingdom of God will happen in the future but also claimed it was already here, it is not an event to come at a certain time but one that comes with individual self realization of justice and goodness in and with all things. Christians knew no one would accept this literal truth so told it in the metaphor of the kingdom of heaven.

Because we are not the One but individual instances of creation in and by the One we are deceived by our perception when things seem dual but are really not, appear good and evil but are really not, seem only all or only One but are really not, the way we live does matter as our individual perception will change from pain or pleasure, from Hell or Heaven depending on how we act. It is all One and One in all but as an individual creation and not the One, our perception is distorted and deceived of not living in the One and living in multiplicity. The way we live influences our perception of living in terms of moving closer to the One or moving/ living further away from the One.

Out of necessity the cosmos was created from God. The cosmos is Beauty. All is one and one is all. As individual beautiful phenomena we are ignorant. Intuition leads to the realization that All is God. One has to realize all is God. Creation emanated out of necessity. All beings strive toward the One. Great things are excellent and rare out of necessity of Being excellent. Ignorant individual beings are created out of necessity and are a beautiful expression. We are created out of necessity as a beautiful expression and our purpose is to return to God. Therefore contemplate and teach the One.

God is always there as one's inner being. We are ignorant born in matter out of necessity.

God is perfect and does not change but creates. It is an unmoved mover. Creation changes which means creation without the realization of God is perceived as imperfect.

The teaching of the Vedanta claims that atman and Brahman are one. If we remove the terms of these things from their historical and cultural routes we can discern that atman is the soul or the mind and Brahma is God or in Neo Platonic terms the One. Vedanta is claiming that the mind is identical with God or the most profound part of the mind is God. God is the cause of consciousness and the mind. The cause of the mind is immaterial. Many modern researchers particularly of western countries of the United States and Europe may disagree with this conclusion. Yet no argument can be given for a conclusion which requires the transcendence of reason to arrive at.

Miscellaneous Aphorisms and Epigraphs

The meaning of life is Beauty, Truth, and Love, therefore we should do Art, Religion, and Philosophy in life.

-Even though most people may not be able to experience god or may not have the divine spark within them as Eckhart put it or they may not have the most profound part of the soul which is Brahman or God within them they still may study or be attracted to their creator which is God and which they are a part of. One way is by attending a religious organization. This is like moths being attracted to light, though they may never experience oneness with God.

-Why must scholars today think that the pursuit of knowledge is never ending and there is no end to knowledge? They are skeptics, relativists, and positivists. They do not realize that the ultimate questions have already been answered such as the meaning of life. People discovered the meaning of life thousands of years ago. Maybe even before then.

-We are done waiting for Godot. Godot never showed up; so we are moving on. Likewise we are done with postmodernism and moving on to better systems. And most people don't pay attention to Godot and postmodernism at all; and live according to their own systems!

-Oh how dishonest, insecure, and petty many people are. Those with problems cannot come to be honest and tell the truth about the way they feel and their problems. People in society are petty towards one another.

-On behalf of theocracy and the Islamic State. They are trying to create the best state they can. The ideal state. Freedom does not necessarily lead to goodness. Promoting goodness with the aid of the state often helps.

-The only justification for imperialism is to make the conquered people a better people and that the ones who conquer are greater than the one's conquered.

-Once one obtains enlightenment of ultimate sacred reality one has reached the end and purpose of life.

-Why teach students to write a three part essay? No published writer ever writes in that format. You say life doesn't matter, I say the One and the Many are the same.

The shadow of nonsense always hangs over those who try to ignore truth.

Face the darkness; and begin the odyssey to overcome it.

Wealth is the fuel of power.

The mind uncensors everything.

There is only one universe.

The Mystical Philosophy

Mysticism is the concept of the mind attaining an experience of an Ultimate Sacred Reality. The ways in which such mystical experiences of ultimate sacred reality are attained, the experiences themselves, and the parallels between different mystical traditions will be described. The terms ultimate sacred reality, union with God, nirvana, enlightenment, and the experience, will be used synonymously. Throughout history there have been many mystics. The validity and nature of Mysticism will be assessed in this book.

One of the fundamental limitations of describing mystical states is that they are beyond language. Mystical experience has often been claimed to be ineffable. This is because one is attempting to describe an experience which is beyond distinctions and multiplicity. Mystical experiences are beyond ordinary human conceptions. Hence an attempt to describe such experiences in language will be full of contradictions. The question may be raised why use language at all to describe an experience which is ultimately ineffable. Through language, one can provide an idea of what a mystical experience is somewhat like. But any linguistic description will not be able to give an account which completely does justice to what the experience is really like.

Aristotle (384-322 BCE) Greek Philosopher who writes that philosophy begins with wonder (Aristotle 692). People wonder about the world and there place in it. They also wonder at the mere fascination of wondering. They want to know the truth about things. As philosophy is the love of wisdom, wisdom is truth but the question arises what is wisdom. It seems that Spinoza's intellectual love of God (Copleston 249) and philosophical love of wisdom are analogous. In fact Spinoza thinks that by obtaining knowledge of God one becomes wise or gains wisdom (Copleston 244). Mystics claim to have gained supreme wisdom and knowledge of God. This is an essential feature of mysticism. According to Plato wisdom is virtue (Copleston 219). Virtue includes the four cardinal virtues described by Plato as justice, courage, moderation, and wisdom (Copleston 220). It seems that the good life and the life of understanding are both wisdom. Morality and understanding are both part of wisdom. Aristotle would agree as theoretical science and practical science both contribute to understanding and happiness (Reeve xvii). Ethics, Metaphysics, and Philosophy of Religion are all closely connected and interrelated as they all express truths about existence. Mysticism is in many ways a unity of ethics, metaphysics, and philosophy of religion.

It may be asked how the conscious subject, and mystics all start out as conscious subjects, realizes freedom within, becomes wise, and thus become mystics. How does the conscious subject stop being determined by passions and desires and become free and wise? The conscious subject realizes he is an individual separate from the group, becomes contemplative, and turns toward inner reflection. This is the beginning of freedom and the path towards becoming wise. Milton wrote long and hard is the path out of darkness leading to light. The path of contemplation and inner reflection is full of much suffering especially when the subject does not know the truth. Ignorance is the cause of suffering, truth and wisdom stop suffering. Mystics have begun their ascetic ways often with inner reflection and contemplation. Sometimes a mystic is an individual and a nonconformist who goes about pursuing his own individual way to truth which brings him to mystical experience. The natural sciences attempt to gain knowledge of the empirical world. When it is claimed that something is scientifically proven this means something has been empirically verified. Science attempts to understand nature by knowledge gained through the senses. We start from knowledge of the senses and from sensual knowledge we reason towards higher things than sensual knowledge and eventually to ultimate things such as the intelligences and the spiritual understanding of everything. Science does not engage in inner contemplation but gains all its knowledge from the external world and the sensual world. This knowledge is the basis to gain higher knowledge. Mystical knowledge is attained through the intellect. Everyone begins with sensual experience and few individuals gain mystical knowledge through the intellect.

The ancients used the term soul to refer to some one's consciousness, the self, and personal identity. Aristotle writes in his "De Anima" (On the Soul) about ones imagination, senses, and perception all of which are aspects of consciousness (Aristotle 534). Consciousness in and of itself is both internal and external, ever realistic and ever idealistic both outward and inward. Consciousness turns inward through contemplation and outward into the world of perceptions. Spinoza wrote thought and extension are two perspectives of the same thing which is substance. The physical and the phenomenal are two perspectives of the same thing which is consciousness. The soul is consciousness, and can be interpreted as the self or some one's personal identity. The Buddha did not think the soul as the self or personal identity existed. Buddha's view is similar to some contemporary theories of personal identity such as that of Parfit who claims relation to ones self as a past person is important. Parfit thinks personal identity is not important or does not matter. Attachment to one's ego comes from the illusion of a particular self. Defense of one's ego and reputation suggests insecurity about the illusory ego one is attached to. Appearances can be deceiving. One should realize one's self or personality is transitory and should not be attached to a particular personality. All selves are transitory. The true self is Brahman and is the self of the wise man. In the spiritual experience one realizes all is good and all change is good. Ultimate Reality does not change but all sensible and phenomenal beings change. The conscious subject must overcome his transitory self to exist as the true self described as Brahman which is the self of the mystic and the self of wisdom.

The relationship between the mind and the body should be considered when describing mystical experience. The mind is not identical to the body and the body is not identical to the mind. The mind and body are related. The feelings and perceptions in the body can affect the mind if the mind lets them. Thoughts and imaginations in the mind can affect the body. Mind and body are interrelated and interconnected. Mind and body are not identical and mind and body are not completely separate entities. Mind is different from body and body is different from mind. Bodies can exist without the mind, and the mind in order to have sense perception must be part of the body. One cannot see, hear, smell, taste, or touch without the necessary body parts. One must have a mind in order to perceive through the senses. One can have a nonfunctional brain, and have no sense perception. The mind and brain are not exactly the same thing or alike and are not completely different. Mind and body are interrelated and interconnected. The body is dependent on the mind to function. The mind is dependent on the body to be conscious of itself. The essence of the soul is the part of the mind that is separate from the body. The essence of the soul is immortal and eternal. The essence of the soul when realized emanates its goodness to the body so the body is usually more beautiful when the essence of the soul is realized. The mind must become independent from the influence of the body through contemplation to realize its essence and thus gain mystical experience.

Through mystical experience one realizes that the essence of one's soul is eternal. The rational part of the mind which is the soul is eternal or immortal. Things in existence will always act rationally and harmoniously according to the metaphysical laws of nature. These laws of nature are harmony and mathematical truths. Nature will always act harmoniously and according to mathematical truths. Harmony and mathematical truths are reasonable and rational and are therefore part of reason. Since these laws of nature are eternal, reason is eternal. Since reason is eternal, the reasonable part of the soul is eternal. Aristotle called this part of the soul the active intellect and Eckhart called it the spark of the soul which is according to Eckhart the part of the soul that is divine (Davies xxv). Consciousness is not eternal and consciousness no longer exists at death, but the rational part of consciousness is eternal. This is what religions mean when it is written "for God so loved the world he gave his only begotten son, for whoever believeth in him shall not perish but have everlasting life" and "Siddhartha Guatama will pass away, but the Buddha will not die". Eternal life is figurative for the conscious state of enlightenment in which the conscious subject no longer perceives time but transcends the illusion of time and comprehends the enlightened aspect of the mind and reality. When he or she knows the divine and rational essence of the soul the person becomes conscious of his or her own immortality (Plato 352). The person realizes the divine and rational part of their soul is immortal and therefore realizes part of them is immortal. What is divine and what is rational is eternal. God is eternal. God is eternal and whoever understands it, their soul shall live forever because it unites with what is eternal.

There are mystics in all of the world's religious traditions. All of the great religions were correct including Hinduism, Buddhism, Taoism, Confucianism, Christianity, Islam, and Judaism. The Bahai faith explicitly states that all religions are expressions of the same truth. When it is said that all the religions are correct it is meant that they all express the same true spiritual experience. They all include accounts of the same mystical experience manifested in different ways. All religions are correct in comprehending the divine and have developed different interpretations of the same thing. They all contain interpretations of the same mystical experience. There is one ultimate sacred reality expressed as God whether one calls it Allah, Yahweh or Jehovah, it is the same thing, the same God, there is one God. Ultimate Sacred Reality has been expressed as all of the major divinities. All of the divinities are identical, God is Allah, Allah is Yahweh, and Yahweh is God. All religions describe one and the same spiritual experience manifested as different interpretations. Many religions have called this higher state of consciousness God, enlightenment, and Brahman. William Blake wrote that all religions are one in that they are all an expression of the poetic genius (Blake 79). The Persian poet Rumi wrote that many roads lead to the one goal which is union with God (Copleston 97). This means that there are many ways a person can attain the higher state of consciousness which can be described as ecstasy or pure bliss and is also a state of complete spiritual understanding of everything. It is also known in non religious philosophical systems such as that of Plotinus as the One, to a lesser extent in Spinoza as knowing substance or the intellectual love of God, and in Hegel's system as absolute spirit. Other non religious interpretations of this spiritual experience are in the philosophies of Plato and Aristotle. Many others have described this state of consciousness in both religious and non religious terms however there are too many to list them all here. I highly recommend The Perennial Philosophy by Aldous Huxley which explains how all religions are interconnected and all are different interpretations of the same spiritual experience. Another book which expresses this same view is John Hick's The Fifth Dimension. In Christian mysticism the experience is described as union with God, in Muslim Sufism it is described as divine intoxication and union with Allah, Buddhism describes it as enlightenment and Nirvana, and Hinduism describes it as becoming one with Brahman. The experience is a phenomenal and spiritual comprehension of all existence. The answer to all possible questions and the meaning of life can only be understood in the state of enlightenment, Nirvana, God, Allah, Yahweh, Brahman, and the One, which are expressions of Ultimate Sacred Reality; they are all interpretations of the same thing. When a person has a mystical experience all questions in existence have been answered in a spiritual way. The experience is the culmination and height of knowledge. All profound questions of existence and life are answered by the mystical experience. One has a profound spiritual understanding of existence.

Many religious texts should be interpreted metaphorically and will be correctly interpreted by mystics. Statements are true when taken in different senses and ways. Religion and Philosophy are two ways of expressing the same truth. The person who has the potential to have or has had spiritual experience of reaching supreme happiness or union with ultimate sacred reality which is the goal will correctly know how to interpret religious texts. One may know how to identify such a person because the person will have a virtuous character, will not indulge and not be disturbed in his or her bodily pleasures and pains, will have no passions and no desires, and will also be reasonable, intelligent, ascetic, patient, and compassionate. The person who has these characteristics is the prophet and philosopher. The wise man and the mystic will know how to correctly interpret religious texts. An example of a passage which should be interpreted metaphorically is 'for God so loved the world he gave his only begotten son, for whoever believeth in him shall not perish but have everlasting life'. Another passage is 'Siddhartha Guatama will pass away, but the Buddha will not die'. The Buddha is the eternal truth, Siddhartha was its embodiment. The true believer will live forever in the experience of ultimate sacred reality. Ultimate Sacred Reality is eternal and timeless and it was expressed in Buddhism and other religions and philosophies. The true believer and the Buddha are similar in that they both contain eternal life. These two passages parallel each other making it evident that there is a connection between Buddhism and Christianity. The son of God and the Buddha are expressions of people who understood the eternal essence of things.

What has been interpreted as an after life or heaven and hell in many religions is actually a metaphorical description of a person's state of consciousness. Heaven is analogous to happiness while Hell is analogous to misery. Those who behave morally are happy and in heaven while those who behave immorally are miserable and in hell. Dante's account of Hell and Heaven in the "Divine Comedy" should be interpreted metaphorically as different states of consciousness. Dying and going to an after life should be interpreted metaphorically as not being able to change the moral or immoral actions one has done and thus goes to a particular state of consciousness. An after life should be interpreted metaphorically as ones state of consciousness after one acts morally or immorally to cause the particular state of consciousness. There is no consciousness after death as one does not have any sense perception because ones brain and body no longer function.

Reincarnation is both true and false. The same personalities reincarnate in people throughout history but the people are different because their memories are different. Throughout history people contain the same personalities because the personalities express the same habits and emotions in all people. There are always variations in people's personalities but they are basically the same. People do not reincarnate into animals, insects, and plants. And animals, plants, and insects do not reincarnate in people. Animals and plants do not have the same rational and conscious faculties as people do. Reincarnation in Hinduism should be interpreted metaphorically in that through ones good and wise deeds one is liberated from life and attains union with Brahman in that their consciousness attains to the highest state of knowing ultimate sacred reality. One perceives and knows ultimate sacred reality in this state. Reincarnation is a metaphor for living an unliberated life of passion and desires. Freedom and liberation from reincarnation result in becoming wise such as the wise man and attaining the state of consciousness known as Ultimate Sacred reality. One being reincarnated as an insect or an animal should be interpreted metaphorically as one becoming less wise and having more desires and passions. The mystics think the righteous will be rewarded and the wicked will be punished. The mystics contain a profound morality as to how to best live one's life happily and righteously.

Some mystics have provided a method as to how to attain mystical experience. The method includes self mortification, nonattachment, asceticism, charity, and chastity. The method to attain mystical experience expressed by the mystics will be described next. For humans to attain the mystical experience of Ultimate Sacred Reality subjectively and psychologically is the one true purpose of life. This can be achieved and once it is achieved everything is understood. To know God is to have an understanding of everything and to know and have the greatest happiness any human can have. To obtain God requires great discipline; it is one of the most difficult things to do. One must have no foolish or lazy thoughts in that one must control the thoughts of one's mind with discipline. One must have tolerance for people. One must have good will and intelligence. One must be able to overcome ones body. This means the mind must have complete control over the body. One cannot let the cravings of one's body control one. One must control and have discipline over ones body to function intelligently.

This means good posture such as a straight back when sitting down with much discipline. One must eat healthy foods that contain a very small amount of meat or no meat at all. The world religions emphasize strict diets because it brings one closer to God. What we eat determines how we feel and think. Eating well causes us to feel and think better. Thinking and feeling well brings us closer to a good state of mind which is a state of mind closer to the Good. One who can control ones body will be closer to God than one who does not control and have discipline over ones body. Controlling one's body brings us closer to the divine because it subordinates the lower to the higher. The mind controls the body, the intellect controls the flesh. If healthy food is not available one must have the discipline to eat unhealthy food without pleasure, controlling the body by the mind.

To obtain Ultimate Sacred Reality is to be free from both bodily pain and pleasure, which results in the ultimate happiness. But one who desires happiness shall not obtain the mystical experience which is ultimate sacred reality. To obtain to the experience one must be free from all desires even the desire to obtain the experience. To have no desires is to be lacking nothing. One wants nothing because one has everything. To obtain God is to have everything and want nothing for oneself. One must act not to obtain happiness but for virtue and virtues purpose. Love everything and hate nothing. Love those you hated in the past and do not hate them anymore. One hates because one feels that ones self has been done wrong to. When one obtains the experience one realizes that no self ever existed at all. One should be patient all the time. Where ever one is one should be patient. To want something now is to lack something now. You have only to realize that you were lacking nothing to begin with. God is always with you all the time and in it contains everything, and nothing for you to wait for. One should not let other people disturb one and try to bully one away from one's quest to obtain the experience. They are ignorant of the truth and do not understand those who do understand. One should have patience and endurance towards them and do not hate them for what they do. One should not act violently or insult them, to do so would be a form of hate and one should never hate but always love, for God is love. To have discipline, patience, and endurance towards people who disturb one, one shall know that there is no situation that cannot be overcome. For every good action the one who does the good action is psychologically rewarded. For every bad action the one who does the bad action is psychologically punished. When one does what is good one feels good and becomes a better person. When one does what is bad one becomes worse and thus feels worse. Those who intentionally disturb one on one's quest to realize their essence will be psychologically punished. One should not take credit for one's good actions. One should do good actions and not see them as something to be rewarded but only as one's duty. A person has faith when the person does not know if there is any reward involved in good actions and does not expect a reward for doing them but does good actions because they are good. Faith in this sense is connected to virtue by doing good actions for no other reason than it is good to do them. Doing selfless good actions for no reward in return is part of faith. By doing the good one becomes the good which generates a good feeling in us which leads to happiness. Many mystics were ignorant of the mystical experience they would attain by doing virtue because it was intrinsically good. And because of their devotion they attained the mystical experience. By doing the good for the sake of goodness one comes to what is intrinsically good. Virtue is an end in itself. Through reason we do what is good which is virtue. Virtue is doing the good through reason. By doing the good we become the good and we feel better which makes us more happy. Though happiness comes from virtue, one should not desire happiness or one may never be fulfilled. To desire means something is lacking in one and when one desires, one only has yet to realize that nothing is lacking in one. There will be many psychological barriers in one's quest to obtain God. One should not spend time foolishly entertaining oneself. To accept life as it comes to us requires wisdom and prudence. We should accept the things we cannot control and not let them grieve us. One must have the discipline and intelligence to overcome these barriers and have a clear mind to obtain God. If all of the above steps are followed at the same time one will realize that nothing is lacking in the present moment which will lead one closer and closer to ultimate sacred reality, ultimate truth, and supreme happiness. One should have faith, let nothing discourage one, have peace and love. This is the method which most mystics use in order to attain their experiences. The method is very ascetic and self mortifying. Many mystics give up all there material possessions in order to live according to truth. One should not be bonded and attached to anything. By giving up all one's material possessions one is not attached to anything which grants one a clearer mind with no bondage and thus makes it easier to contemplate and attain union with God. The mystics give up every material possession and familial connection they have and devote their minds completely to goodness, beauty, truth, and love which they have called God, Brahman, Allah, and many other terms.

The life of wisdom is the same as the life of the mystic and the wise man. The life of wisdom is a life according to the virtues of courage, moderation, prudence, discipline, magnanimity, and justice. In order to be courageous one must know the difference as Aristotle claims between cowardice and rashness. In order to be moderate one must not indulge in excessive amounts of anything and one must not take too little of anything. For example one must not eat too much and one must not eat too little. One must take only what is necessary to lead a good life. In order to be wise one must be prudent or cautious in what one does. Confucius thought the superior man is always aware of his surroundings. The cautious and wise man (man includes both men and women) is always aware of how he behaves and acts. He also knows which situations to avoid by using reason to analyze their consequences. For example, the wise and prudent man knows not to get drunk and gamble all his money away as that will most likely have unattractive consequences in the future. The wise man has discipline and organization as he thinks clearly and organizes his thoughts. He also controls his mind in that he controls his thoughts. The wise man does not care for material possessions and has few material possessions (only those that are needed necessarily). The wise man controls his body in that he does not indulge in the desires of the body such as eating excessive food and controls his sexual urges. The wise man has no desires at all. He is not disturbed by pain and does not rejoice in the ordinary use of the term pleasure. The wise man's pleasure is being wise. He also does not let things that may be uncomfortable to his body bother him such as hot and cold weather. In these ways the wise man is very Stoic. The wise man has patience. Patience is a virtue. Everyone should be patient. The wise man has no pride. It may be true that the wise man is better than the non wise person but the wise man has no pride. Everyone has the potential to become wise. The wise man is magnanimous as he does not let unfortunate things that happen to him upset or disturb him. For example if his house burnt down and he lost all his money, even if he lost a body part he would still not be angry, not upset, and not disturbed. The wise man controls his passions and emotions. The wise man does not become angry or afraid. He is governed by reason and not by the emotions. Spinoza was right when he wrote one should not be controlled by the passions (Copleston 244). Spinoza was also right when he suggested that virtue is right reason (Copleston 248). The wise man is just in that he is honest and impartial. The wise man does all of these things because he knows they are good to do in themselves. He does not act for any reward. He knows that virtue is its own reward in that happiness exists in wisdom. He knows because he has looked within himself and contemplated with right reason what the best things are to do. The best things are what make him most God like. Aristotle was right when he wrote that we should strive as much as we can to be Gods (Aristotle 1108). Pythagoras writes in his "Golden Verses" that by being wise one becomes a God (Pythagoras 9). Epicurus claims that we have the ability to become Gods. Boethius also wrote that the good person is the truly happy person and becomes a God through goodness (Boethius 106). By being wise the wise man becomes a better person and becomes a God. The conduct of the wise man results in mystical experience. The wise man, the ascetic, and the mystic are the same. The mystic has the same qualities and traits which the wise man has.

When it is stated the wise man becomes a God he does not become a God in the sense of his body transforming into something supernatural that can fly or do other physical impossibilities. However his body becomes stronger as he becomes stronger by being wiser. He becomes a God in the sense that he no longer lets worldly things such as pleasure and pain and desires have any effect on him. He is so far above and beyond common ordinary people who are concerned with their worldly pursuits. He also behaves very differently than other people. He does not express or have discontent when unfortunate things happen to him. He does not have any desire for material possessions and does not consume as most people do. Being indifferent to pleasure and pain the wise man seems very strange through the perspective of most people. The wise man is usually an individual who does not conform to the group of ordinary people. Most people may not understand the wise man which may lead to his persecution which happened in the cases of wise men such as Jesus and Socrates. The wise man is very rare and most people do not attain a state of wisdom. It is very difficult to attain the state of wisdom as one must do all the things to be wise stated above and have no desires, not even a desire to be wise. One must be virtuous for no reward and not for any desire but because being virtuous is good in itself. It is true what Spinoza wrote that all excellent things are difficult and rare (Spinoza 271). Great things are rare which makes them great.

Loving God and serving God are really the same thing. One does virtuous actions because one loves God and serves God and one loves God by meditating about God and becoming one with God. One realizes God is realized in one all the time after the experience and one may serve God for the rest of the time. After one attains the mystical experience, one is always embodying the divine and liberated in the world. But meditation which is prayer serves to bring us close to the experience. The experience is good in itself and one realizes that all existence is good in the world. The experience reveals that all existence is good. One does the good and is the good in the world after the experience. Doing the good and being the good are the same thing. The mystics claim that everything is good which is a realization from the experience although one does not know of the intrinsic goodness of existence if one has not had a mystical experience.

By doing what is good, virtuous, and moral one becomes the good. By abstaining from bodily pleasures, self control, eating healthily, great discipline and control of mind and body, patience, compassion, simplicity, nonattachment to material things, love of all things, selfless acts, humility and lack of pride, and subjugating one's passions and emotions, doing good acts because they are good in themselves, one attains the spiritual experience. One becomes the good and is the good by doing these things. One becomes God and is God by doing these things. The purpose, goal and meaning of life is to be God.

The experience itself is being in an ultimate light. Entirely within love, ecstasy, peace, serenity, tranquility, harmony, happiness, and all of these things are one. They are all words expressing the same experience. There is absolutely no pain and no evil in the experience but supreme joy, bliss, and completely supreme non corporeal pleasure. One knows and comprehends enlightenment through the mind, although one's sense perception in the state of enlightenment is different than in ordinary sense perception without enlightenment. One sees things as intrinsically beautiful, all perceived things are full of value. A person who has the experience completely understands all of nature and the harmony of nature. Through the experience a person understands all things. One realizes through the experience that existence is good just by existing. Through knowing this magnificent vision one knows all things.

The experience of Ultimate sacred Reality itself reveals the beauty of all existence. One who describes the experience itself to others will not give to others the actual experience. Others who have not had the experience must have it themselves to know what the mystic who has had the experience is talking about. Language of the experience does not reveal what the experience is truly like. One who is taught about the experience but does not have the experience ones self usually will not live a virtuous life and a good life just because someone has described the experience and the good life to them. According to an old Chinese proverb to know and not to do is not to know. One who knows about the experience but has never had the experience will not really know what the experience is like. Although one will have a reasonable idea of what the experience is like from descriptions of it.

One of the fundamental questions which has been asked by all human kind is what is the meaning of life. Mystics claim to have answered this question. The sentence can be rearranged so that it states what makes life meaningful or why are we here. The best answer to this question is beauty, truth, and love. Beauty, truth, and love are the meaning of life. Beauty, truth, and love are the most meaningful things in human life. And these three things are one. According to Keats beauty and truth are one and the same thing (Keats 2). One may notice that beauty, love, and truth are analogous to Hegel's three methods of obtaining knowledge of absolute spirit which are Art, Religion, and Philosophy. These three things are one because the aesthetic feeling of the beautiful is the same feeling of true goodness. And wanting to do the good is due to love of being. If one did not love beings one would not want to do good for them. This feeling of the beautiful, the true, the good, and love culminate in a higher state of consciousness. This higher state of consciousness has been called ultimate sacred reality. Aquinas wrote that the greatest happiness is for the mind to attain God (Aquinas (cover)). Aquinas also thought this higher state of consciousness existed. This experience of a higher state of consciousness should not be taken as a proof of God's existence. It is a proof to the subject or person who has the experience. It is not a proof in the sense that it can be written down with premises and a conclusion that God exists. The proof is not public and is very subjective as it is only a proof to the person who has the experience. The experience occurs in Mysticism as all the religious traditions of the world contain similar accounts of the experience. Schopenhauer wrote that because there is no proof of his experience the mystic is unable to convince people that his experience is true, the philosopher on the other hand is able to convince as the philosopher provides arguments and reasons which support the conclusion (Schopenhauer 611). This does not make the mystics claims any less true, although it does make them unconvincing and very difficult to believe for someone who has never had the experience. In William James's Varieties of Religious Experience countless examples are given of people who have had similar experiences to the one described above. After one attains this experience there seems to be nothing left to do as Plotinus writes after one attains union with the One he is liberated from all worldly pursuits and flies from the Alone to the Alone (Plotinus 360). The experience is similar to Plato's allegory of the cave in which the freed individual comes out of the cave and sees the sun. This symbolizes the person seeing the Truth and having the experience of knowing the Form of the

Beautiful as written in Plato's Symposium. After the person has this experience of knowing the Form of the Good and the Beautiful he goes back to the cave to teach the others the Truth of what he has learned. It seems this is what is left for the person who has the experience to do. The person must return to the illusory world to teach people the truth. Even if these people mistreat and kill the enlightened individual he still must try to guide them to the truth. Once enlightened individuals and philosophers succeed in enlightening all people (which will most likely never happen) all of humanity will simply exist in the greatness and perfection of existence. Most people do not attain truth and enlightenment and must do so out of their own efforts and not through constant encouragement. The philosopher or enlightened person still has an obligation to teach and encourage people to pursue and attain truth however the enlightened person has already attained truth. The enlightened person has fulfilled his or her purpose in life. Still this person should continue teaching others to pursue the life of wisdom.

The meaning of life cannot fully be comprehended in language but the meaning of life in words is beauty, truth, and love. The meaning of life is beauty, truth, and love. And these three are one. When one obtains enlightenment one realizes that one already contained the meaning of life in every moment in existence. Once enlightenment is obtained philosophy and theology and everything else is over, all of life's questions have been answered. It is not factual but spiritual wisdom that leads to absolute truth. It is impossible to know all the facts there are in the world but it is possible to have a spiritual understanding of everything. The purpose of human life is to become one with the divine, with God (which is beauty, truth, love and goodness in one). The meaning of life is realized all the time which is revealed in the experience. Mystics of all periods have a profound love for existence which is revealed to them in their experience of knowing all things as beauty, truth, and love. This is the source of pantheism in mysticism. The mystic experiences all things as God and sees God in all things. All things in existence are perceived as beautiful, lovely, and sacred. Since the mystic is experiencing God when he perceives all things as sacred and since the experience of God is the spiritual experience of all things in omniscience spiritually conceived, the mystic realizes that all is God. Physics wants to find the theory of everything. People such as Buddha, Plotinus, Hindu sages, Daoist sages, and others already discovered the meaning of life and the theory of everything a long time ago.

Mystics write of intrinsic beauty of the cosmos. According to the mystics matter is constantly in flux, however, ultimate sacred reality is eternal and never changes. Everything changes and everything stays the same and it is all part of one divine cosmic dance. The world changes, but the ideas and states remain eternal. Mystics write that diversity is conducive to appreciate and become one with the divine because it displays the infinite beauty of the world which is a creation of the divine being. Loving the beauty of the world is conducive to attaining mystical experience.

This may not be very satisfying in scientific terms but is as close as I can think of to describe what pure energy is. Through the subjective experience described in this book one comes to know what pure energy is which is a manifestation of love and beauty emanating from themselves. Pure energy is love and beauty and all things are love and beauty. Harmony is in all things as all things are energy which is love and beauty. Love and Beauty and Harmony are the same thing. Reason is the good which is truth. Love is the good which is truth, and the experience of it is beautiful. Reason, The Good, Truth, Love, and Beauty are identical.

In the mystical experience it is revealed that all is one universal. Universals exist though some are inseparable from their particulars. One example of universals is numbers and formulas of mathematics. Mathematical entities do not have any particular existence materially or ontologically in nature, yet they exist. Engineering proves they exist and can be applied to nature. These mathematical entities must be universals as they are not merely names, and they are not merely mental constructs as they apply to nature. Further, they exist separately from particular things and are true by themselves as one does not have to know about them in order for them to exist and be true. Therefore universals exist in mathematics. Another universal is harmony. Any existing thing taken into consideration behaves harmoniously. All physical things act and move in accordance to natural laws. For example a rock thrown upwards will fall down in accordance with gravity. Therefore since harmony is not merely a name, and it is not merely a mental construct, it is a universal. In fact mathematics and harmony are the same things. Mathematics is logical (as Russell's logicism claims (Copleston 438)) and harmonic. They are both universals as they are applied to all things and exist separately from all things. Another universal which is a universal and in some cases exists separately from particulars is being. Everything that exists (including nothing as shown above) has one thing in common, Being. Everything that exists is being. Being is a universal and a universal that can in the case of other universals be separated from particulars. Being is not merely a name and not merely a mental construct as things exist independently of the mind. Some of these things which can exist independently of the mind are mathematical truths. Mathematics exists and is a universal Being. Part of existence is universals such as Mathematical truths which exist separately from particulars, and the universal being exists in particular things that exist such as trees and many other things that exist. Existence is a universal. Being is existence. All things whether they be particulars or universals such as Harmony and Mathematical truths contain the universal Being. Part of Being satisfies the requirement that universals exist separately from particular things because universals such as Harmony and Mathematical truths exist. As Harmony and Mathematical truths have immaterial existence and the universal Being exists in them, part of the Universal Being has immaterial existence. Being is the ultimate universal as it applies to all things both immaterial such as Harmony and Mathematical truths, and particular beings such as trees and many other things that exist. Being is the universal that exists in all particulars and universals.

When one realizes the truth of all things in enlightenment one realizes the truth, the impossible paradox, the universal contradiction that all is one and one is all. In any state of consciousness one is already at enlightenment since existence and nothingness, one and all at enlightenment (which is the realization of reality with no illusions) are realized to be one and the same. God is everywhere, but we find god in the deepest realm of the human heart. Not directed solely towards another person, but towards all existence and nothingness. When one obtains enlightenment one realizes one can completely achieve and fulfill ones purpose in life without having to do anything. Ones purpose in life is achieved and fulfilled completely simply by existing! Complete wisdom and goodness is realized in union with God or Ultimate Sacred Reality. There is wisdom and goodness and happiness outside of the experience but it is realized fully and to the greatest degree in the experience.

The experience is beyond language. In order to truly know the experience one must have the experience ones self. In order to attain the experience one must have great discipline and self control, patience, and one must realize that every moment is an end in itself which means one will realize that there is really nothing to wait for. One is always full and complete. But to attain the experience one must go through this process. One must have no desires at all. One must be virtuous and do good and virtuous things for no reward but because virtue and goodness are good in themselves. One must not be attached to any material possessions. One must not be greedy and not have any sexual desires. Wealth and sex are in the end unsatisfying and unfulfilling. One must control one's passions and be free from destructive emotions. One must not be attached to a particular personality.

The One is always present in the many. A person realizes this when the person experiences ultimate sacred reality. One realizes that one was always perfect and existence was always perfect when one experiences Ultimate Sacred Reality. A person contained perfection within the persons self all along. The person just did not know about it before the person experienced Ultimate Sacred Reality. Plato was right when he thought the truth is always in a person waiting to be discovered by the person. The truth is Ultimate Sacred Reality which is equivalent to God which is Plato's Idea of the Good. Every person has the potential to experience

Ultimate Sacred Reality within the person's self. Once one experiences Ultimate Sacred Reality one realizes that everything is perfect and was always perfect. After the experience the person realizes Ultimate Sacred Reality and God is in everything always. The One (God) is all. God manifests itself in all particular things such as trees and chairs and even feces. In the state of enlightenment all particular things are beautiful and perfect as an expression of God manifesting itself in all things. And all is One (all particular things are part of God). In Ultimate Sacred Reality or the experience of God, the subject who has the experience comprehends that all particular things are part of God. The experience is a spiritual understanding of everything which culminates in one experience. The experience of the One includes a spiritual understanding of all particular things. All particular things are comprehended in the One. The One is the many and the many are the One. All in One and One in all. One is All and All is One. I realize that this is very difficult to believe. The person who has the experience knows it is true and those who do not have the experience do not know that it is true. Separation of God from all things came about as one did not see God in all things and only in the experience. Theism arose as the universal experience was separated from everything else. Theism is true outside the subjective experience as one perceives particular things outside and separate from the experience. Pantheism and Panentheism are both true. Pantheism literally means all is God which means all particular things contain God, God is in all things (One in All). Panentheism literally means all is in God which means when a person has the experience of Ultimate Sacred Reality which is the experience of God, the person comprehends a spiritual understanding of everything. The person realizes that all particular things are understood in God and God is the experience. As all things are understood in God, all is in God (All in One). The experience affirms both Pantheism and Panentheism as mirror images of each other. Parmenides was correct when he said the One is. Parmenides meant the One is the true reality. Xenophanes, the teacher of Parmenides also thought the One is God. Outside of the experience which is the experience of the One people do not experience true reality. As Parmenides said being and truth are equivalent which means being in the conscious state of experiencing the One is true being. The true being is the experience of the One. Not experiencing the One is partial being and not completely true being. As experiencing the One is experiencing true being, not experiencing the One is an illusion in that a person does not experience true being. However since All is One and One is All every person is always in a state of true being but does not know and does not realize they are.

Parmenides' One is the same thing as Spinoza's Substance. For Spinoza all that exists is Substance which is God. According to Parmenides all that really exists is the One. According to the teacher of Parmenides, Xenophanes, the One is God.

Therefore both Spinoza and Parmenides think that all that exists is God or the One. The only thing that is real is this universal Being.

The question has arisen as to whether possible worlds exist. Recent philosophers have different ideas on this issue. Some think possible worlds are real in that they exist. Others think possible worlds are not real because they are not actual. Possible worlds are merely potential and not actual. But neither answers the question which is could things have been otherwise than they are now. If things had been different we would be wondering if they could have been different in that possible world. As has been written above existence itself is necessary. The initial conditions of existence may have to be different in order for another world to be actual. Different initial conditions must be needed or human beings would have to possess free will in the sense that they are self caused. If human beings are free there are an infinite number of possible worlds. It has been written above most human beings are determined by being controlled by their passions and desires and are therefore not free. Leibniz claimed that the actual world is the best of all possible worlds (Copleston 312-313). If God exists and is as Leibniz would say a truth of reason (meaning necessarily exists), he would make the world the best of all possible worlds and no other possible worlds could exist (Copleston 282-283). I can imagine myself existing in another possible world but the world would not be real or actual.

Perhaps possible worlds exist potentially (meaning they do not exist in reality) but not actually. Instances in one's individual life could have been otherwise but not large instances such as the physical universe, the world, and historical movements. Contingency and necessity are really the same things. The more one acts in accordance to the universal the closer we become to necessary being. The more we act in accordance to the particular the closer we come to contingent being. Instances in one's individual life could have been otherwise but when one has a spiritual experience one realizes that everything that happens happens necessarily. All that is and happens exists necessarily. At the ultimate divine level a particular instance could have happened otherwise and it would still be equally as perfect as if it happened another way. The ultimate divine level which is God and Ultimate Sacred Reality could not have happened otherwise and is the only thing that could not have happened otherwise. This divine level applies to all particular instances that happen and could have been otherwise. If the particular instances were otherwise than they are they would be equally as perfect no matter what they were with regards to the divine level. The closer things are to the divine level such as initial conditions which are close to the divine level, the more necessary they are and the more they could not have been otherwise. The more particular an event is such as walking, the more contingent the event is and could have been otherwise. Ultimate sacred reality is necessary being.

When one experiences Ultimate Sacred Reality time ceases to exist in the experience. Since there is no time and one is at union with God, one lives in eternity and has eternal life. One arrives at the state which is a realization that time no longer exists. What one perceives as time is motion in space. Many people say they know what time is but when asked to give a definition of it they cannot do so. One conception of time is that of constant movement towards the future. Augustine himself was puzzled over time as he realized the future does not exist yet and the past no longer exists (Augustine 74-75). According to Augustine all we have is a very short point of present between future and past (Augustine 74-75). Augustine concluded that time is an illusion (Augustine 74-75). Another philosopher, Mc Taggart claimed that time is unreal as the concepts of past, present, and future imply a contradiction (Copleston 246). Another concept of time is that of no past or future but an eternal present. Things are always now and never in the past or future. But if we take time out of existence altogether everything would stop. There would be no motion. Everything would be stuck in the present and would not be able to move towards the future. My definition of time is motion in space. If there is no motion, there would be no time. One may object by claiming one does not move sometimes and time persists. The molecules ones body is made up of are still moving. If time is motion and there wasn't anything that could move, then there would be no time. Now, the motion of moving objects can be reduced to energy. Therefore, if there was no energy there would be no time because there would be no motion. The cause of all motion is energy. One may object by claiming that moving objects in space have no energy, yet they move. This objection is refuted in two ways, first the cause of the movement contained energy. The object could have been moved by the energy of gravity. Secondly, by Einstein's famous equation all matter and thus all objects contain energy because matter is equivalent to energy. Therefore the cause of all motion is energy. Motion itself is energy. This means that if nothing existed, there would be no motion, therefore, there would be no time. A moment consists in infinity and infinity consists in a moment. All is in a moment and the One is in every moment. Time is illusory. I will now turn to the origin of existence.

One of the fundamental questions of philosophy is why is there something rather than nothing. When one thinks about it, it makes much more sense if nothing existed rather than something existing. If nothing existed, there would be no causes as there are no things. Is it true that there is such a thing as nothing or a void? Does nothing exist? If there is a void, which means there is nothing, then nothing exists. The void exists which does not include any thing, therefore no thing exists. But it is paradoxical to say that nothing exists because by nothing we mean non existence. But a void exists, and since a void is nothing then nothing exists. Existence is implicitly contained in nothing or nothingness which is the same thing. Therefore, nothing is something. Because nothing exists, it does not make any sense to speak of nothing without something to compare it to. Without something, there would be no nothingness. In order for nothing to be, something had to be because nothing by itself implies that there is something that makes nothing what it is. In order for nothing to exist, something must exist. Something must have come into being for there to be nothing. In order for something to exist, nothing must exist, and in order for nothing to exist, something must exist. Nothing implies something, and something implies nothing. Without something, there is no nothing, and without nothing, there is no something. If nothing is not a proper term as it is a negation of a thing, consider the term void. Nothing exists as the void. Now all existent things are something. There is the void as we can point to places in space where there is no thing, therefore the void exists. A void exists as something, which is a void. Therefore, nothing exists as something, nothing and something are inseparable. The Chinese sage Chang Tsai was right when he claimed there is no such thing as nonexistence (Capra 223). The religious sutras were correct in stating form is emptiness and emptiness is form (Capra 223). Something is nothing and nothing is something. One may claim that nothing being something satisfies the condition of something existing and void as something does not have to bring about non void. But void cannot exist by itself as something because there would be nothing to compare it to as void so it would not be void. Therefore non void must exist for void to exist. It is a logical contradiction to say there is nothing by itself or something by itself. One cannot have one without the other. Nothing must exist and no cause is required for nothing to exist. Something must exist because nothing would be a meaningless term without something to compare it to. But as has been shown, in order for nothing to exist, something must exist as there is no void without something that makes the void no thing. Therefore, by the very fact that there is nothing, something came into being because there was nothing. Nothing must exist for something to exist. It was a logical necessity that something come into being out of nothing. This is an argument for creatio ex nihilo (creation out of nothing). Something came from nothing in accordance with reason. Existence was created out of nothing because of the nothing and out of love that is existence through the nothing. Existence is the culmination of one divine light that came out of nothing which had to be. It had to be because in order for nothing to exist, something must exist.

The alternative to creation out of nothing is an infinite regress of causes. According to this theory there is no first cause but an infinite regress of causes. The natural question to this theory is what got the regress going. The answer must be either nothing, it was always there, or a first cause. An infinite series of causes could not be the answer since another cause would precede that cause in an infinite regress and the question arises what is the cause of the infinite regress. Claiming an infinite regress of causes does not show how the infinite regress could exist. The infinite regress could not have always existed in time with no cause because the questions arise how and why does it exist. There is no logical explanation why there is an infinite regress. An infinite regress forces one to consider the cause of the regress and how the infinite regress came about. The only possible answer to this question is that a first cause caused all the other causes. Existence and time simultaneously came out of nothing. Time is motion in space which is essential to causation. Thus the source of the infinite regress and the beginning of causes have the same solution, they were caused by nothing. As has been argued above something came out of nothing. All things that exist are energy and if there is no energy there is no motion which means there is no time. Now anything that exists contains energy as all that exists is energy. Energy caused motion by its very nature of being energy, as all energy is in flux, and this caused the beginning of time.

Some have referred to the experience as nothing, emptiness, and boundless openness. God is dependent on nothing. Some Buddhists have spoken of the experience of emptiness. Pseudo Dionysius writes of the darkness above the light and some Taoist thinkers have written about the dark learning. This is another expression for the experience of God which is enlightenment. Ultimately, being and nothing are the same.

God is both being and nothing. The Om of the Indian Religions tries to express the experience as nothingness which is complete non attachment to anything. This gives rise to complete tranquility and peace in nothingness which is something. Language is limited because it brings about distinctions between being and nonbeing, something and nothing whereas in ultimate reality there are no distinctions and no multiplicity. Language always implies distinctions and multiplicity to separate one thing from another. As soon as one labels something one has labeled it as distinct from something else whereas in Ultimate Sacred Reality, there are no distinctions and no multiplicity. The experience is described as nothingness because it cannot ultimately be expressed in language. All things come from nothing. The state reveals that one should have complete non attachment to anything. In the experience of nothingness samsara and nirvana are revealed to be one and the life of the saint and the life of the sinner are ultimately one because everything comes out of this emptiness which is boundless openness. Schopenhauer claimed all of existence to be nothing. Ultimately the One and nothingness are the same. All existence is derived from nothing. All existence is ultimately One as described in the writings on Parmenides and pantheism and this One which is something fulfills the logical necessity that in order for nothing to exist something must exist. Nothing is something and what exists is reduced ultimately to nothing.

Most of the universe is full of nothing. All language which attempts to describe the experience and the experience of nothing is deficient because the experience is beyond linguistic distinctions. Complete nonattachment to everything including one's self is revealed in the experience which has been described as nothing. All is One and One is All is revealed in the experience. The author of the Theologia Germanica wrote that All is One and One is All in God. One can arrive at the conclusion that One is All through reason. It is a very unique nothingness which is something. Being which is nothing, it is ultimately indestructible. Something is nothing. In the experience of nothingness it is revealed that samsara and nirvana are the same. The sacred and profane, the saint and the sinner are all identical. Something comes out of nothing and ultimately nothing is something. All existence is ultimately nothing which is something and gives rise to all phenomena. Emptiness in Buddhism claims that there is no permanent self and there is no permanent being. No moment is privileged over any other moment, they are all the same. There is no substantial existence. All phenomena come out of nothing. Nothing is something. Non being is Being. Hegel proclaimed that logically through a similar form of reasoning being and nonbeing are identical. The experience of nothing is the realization that all things are one and there is no difference between samsara and nirvana, the life of the sinner and the life of the saint. One should still be moral and good because being good is in accordance to this nature. The experience of nothing is the experience of all things as their ultimate ground. All things are the same which arise out of this nothing and are ultimately, essentially nothing. The One is nothing and all things are nothing. In the supreme experience this is realized. The very essence in which existence takes place is based on silence and nothingness. Through deep silence of infinite multitudes springs forth creation. When the mind is set in the correct frame of reference it can explore things such as the greatest mysteries of life through the deepest manifestations of the soul. All things are one and once an individual truly understands the nature of this concept great understanding will emerge. A person cannot learn all of the concrete facts in life but can learn everything spiritually. The knowledge being discussed is the deep and incomprehensible by words knowledge of God. God is in everything and is all around us. God which is Ultimate Sacred Reality is beyond gender distinctions. God is not a he or a she but an it.

Schopenhauer, at the end of his World as Will and Representation, wrote that the universe, with all its galaxies, stars and planets, is nothing (Schopenhauer 411-412). He also writes that the ascetic, who has denied the Will to Live, views the world as nothing, which is why he abandons the world to lead a life of meditation and internal reflection (Schopenhauer 411). People who are still subjugated by the Will to Live think of the world as everything and are caught up in the world constantly engaging in futile worldly pursuits (Schopenhauer 412). The people who are controlled by the Will to Live perceive the ascetic life as nothing and not worth pursuing (Schopenhauer 412). As has been written above, nothing is something so the ascetic and ordinary people both view the same thing, but one group views it as something and the other as nothing. Schopenhauer doubtless thinks the ascetic who has denied the Will to Live has the correct interpretation of the world (Schopenhauer 411-412). The ascetic sees things as they truly are beyond the illusion of the world (Schopenhauer 412).

Have no fear, have no anger, have no anxiety, do not worry, do not be afraid, despite everything, everything is all right (Hindu Proverb). All suffering is because of ignorance. Ignorance leads to fear and suffering. True happiness cannot and will never be a source coming from other people and external things. We become omnipotent when we are able to cope, handle, and deal with any and every situation. When there is no situation that will bother us no matter how bad the situation is, we become omnipotent. The free spirit can overcome all desires and all situations. True happiness cannot and will never be a source coming from other people and external things. "Conquer your passions and you conquer the world" (Hindu proverb), the proverb means if one is no longer controlled by the emotions and desires, one will be able to deal with any situation in the world and not be bothered with any situations in one's life. Descartes meant the same thing when he wrote "Conquer yourself rather than the world". One should be wise rather than literally conquer the world. If one literally conquers the world and is not wise, the person will still have passions and desires which will make the person unhappy. The wise person is happy whether the wise person literally conquers the world or does not literally conquer the world.

Responses to Objections

Now a series of objections to mysticism will be discussed. It may be asked, "How does one know one has such an experience?" The experience itself is so sublime it is self affirming; one knows that one is having such an experience. One may say someone could have such an experience by taking drugs or by sexual pleasure. Taking drugs or sexual pleasure are not based on any moral merit or wisdom which the experience is based on. One has complete spiritual understanding of everything in the experience and does not have this true understanding merely by taking drugs or by sexual pleasure. There is no moral merit and wisdom merely in taking drugs and sexual pleasure.

It may be objected that the proclaimed adherents of these religions do not consider other religions to be correct. A follower of one religion will consider all other religions to be incorrect. Most often the followers of other religions do not live by the doctrines of their proclaimed religion. Many proclaimed Christians for example will not live a life of humility and charity. Many followers of religions fight people of other religions thinking they are evil and follow a false God. If they were true adherents of their religion they would love others despite what religion people follow. Many people in other religions do not understand that other religions have the same ethical doctrines and all prescribe to the existence of a benevolent deity. They do not realize that different people in different historical and cultural circumstances can arrive at the same truth.

One must be good at ethics in order to be good at metaphysics. The spiritual experience cannot be attained unless one is a good person. By taking drugs one will not attain the full experience because it loses its value from easily taking drugs. Virtue enables one to attain a higher state of consciousness which is the spiritual experience. In order to have any direct experience of the spiritual experience a person must be a good person. Knowledge of the One is attained through the spiritual experience and only secondarily and very indirectly through the study of Metaphysics.

If someone claimed to have such an experience today he or she would be called insane. Many people today would think the wise man as described in the section above is insane. Knowing and acting according to true reality is not insane. Most ordinary people would be insane by the standards of wisdom described in the above section. Therefore the wise man who has the subjective experience and expresses his wisdom and experience is not insane and most ordinary people with their desires and passions are insane compared to the wise man.

If all is a benevolent deity, then why is there evil? There are many seeming evils, inequalities, and unfairness in life. Technology is making it more difficult to achieve enlightenment. There are more sounds and possibilities that technology brings which the individual must overcome. One must overcome all of them to gain enlightenment. One must not let the evils bother one and one should always be the best and most virtuous person one can be. If one does this one will be happy, wise, and understand despite the seeming evils. One of the best ways mystics have overcome the evils is to live an ascetic life outside of society.

Evil is due to human passion and desire, it is better that people must overcome passion and desire than if they did not have these evils to overcome. If there was no passion and no desire there would be no goodness either. There must be evil things such as passion and desire in order for good things to exist. If humans always performed good actions and there was no passion and no desire, these good actions would be meaningless and valueless as humans would have no choice in performing the actions and there would be no good intentions. Now all humans have the potential to be wise and free through reason. But most never realize their potential because they have become accustomed to the way things are and are fearful because they are ignorant of the way they could be. Evil is something to be overcome. Without evil one could not attain enlightenment as there would be no challenges the individual must go through which are necessary to be worthy of enlightenment. Evil makes it difficult to attain enlightenment, but without this difficulty and evil as an obstacle, enlightenment would not be as great as it is because it would be easier to obtain. If enlightenment was easy to obtain, it would not be so sublime nor would it be enlightenment. One can overcome evil by not letting evil and evil things disturb one's self. As evil is only evil in that it does harm, if one does not let evil harm or disturb one's self psychologically, evil cannot harm the person who does not let the evil disturb himself or herself psychologically. One cannot avoid physical evil such as losing a leg, but if one does not let physical evil such as losing a leg bother one psychologically at all, one is not harmed by evil. Even if one is being severely tortured, one can escape the evil if one does not let the evil of being tortured bother or disturb one's self psychologically. I could be in terrible pain, but if I do not let the pain bother me psychologically I don't let the evil harm me. One can overcome evil if one does not let evil bother one psychologically. In the enlightened state of consciousness it is certain that evil cannot harm one and thus evil ceases to exist. Evil is just a lack of good, a lack of Truth, a lack of Beauty, and a lack of Love. When one perceives evil, evil exists as nonbeing. Everything is God and nothing is the Devil. The Devil is composed of nonexistence which constitutes ignorance and lack of knowledge of God.

A person cannot willingly commit evil actions because whatever action a person commits will be directed toward what a person thinks is good. All humans act toward what they think is good. An action must be motivated by love and not hate in order to be truly good. Doing evil things because they are evil in themselves would destroy us. It would remove us from the harmony and the good which makes us happy. Evil actions harm one psychologically and good actions are rewarded psychologically. Evil actions make one miserable. Mystics think that a higher power will ultimately punish evildoers and reward the righteous.

Some may claim the study of this subjective experience is not empirical because it cannot be observed publicly by any group of people at any time. It is true that the experience cannot be observed publicly at any time. To study the experience one studies the accounts of the experience by people who claim to have the experience. It is true that the accounts of the experience are not the experience itself. By saying I have experienced ecstasy one does not deliver to the other person the actual experience of ecstasy. However the study of the experience is very empirical as it gathers and analyzes the accounts or data of subjects who claim to have the experience. All knowledge is empirical even knowledge that is claimed to be a priori because one must experience doing a priori knowledge. There was never a rationalist who did not use experience and there was never an empiricist who did not use reason.

Henri Bergson distinguished between static and dynamic religion in which static religion is the religion of most people who go to church and call themselves a certain religion but do not live an authentically religious life (Copleston 210). Kierkegaard claimed that people who call themselves Christian are not true Christians because they do not lead the authentically ascetic religious life (Copleston 339) (ascetic here is taken in its religious sense, but it is possible for one to be an ascetic and not be religious). Dynamic religion is the authentic religious life of the ascetic as described in mysticism (Copleston 210). In this essay I have been mainly describing religion in the dynamic sense of the term. I do realize that most people act and think towards religion in its static sense. However the founders of religions such as the Buddha and Jesus Christ initiated religions based on the dynamic aspect.

If humans do not have free will then they could not have any power in becoming wise. Determinism is true to an extent. Most people are physically determined. We are determined by our environment in that we cannot walk through a concrete wall and we cannot fly by ourselves. Most people are governed by their desires and are determined. But there are very rare exceptions in which a person is truly free. We cannot be physically free to fly or walk through concrete walls, but we gain inner freedom through wisdom. The wise man is free in that he is not governed by desire or the emotions. He is not determined by ordinary human life which makes him free. In a sense his wisdom makes him determined to be wise but since he is not subject to so many things that determine human thought and behavior he is as free as it is possible to be free. Real freedom comes from self control and not being controlled by the passions as well as not being controlled by desire. Reason makes us free. The wise man is free.

This state of consciousness cannot be learned from books, it is something which only extraordinary individuals achieve. Once this state is obtained everything is understood in existence and outside of existence. The person who achieves this state realizes that he or she was actually in the state of consciousness all along but only had to realize it for one's self. One does not have to read anything to attain the greatest spiritual experience. God can be realized within. One must look within ones self to attain the experience. All books and everything external is unnecessary and secondary to attaining the experience. Something can be learned from every event whether fortunate or unfortunate. Primordial man could have attained enlightenment and he would have attained it without the use of books. Books can be used as guides to enlightenment but the attainment of enlightenment must be based on the merit of the individual who attains it which sometimes takes the form of a thought process which leads to a state of grace. Books can be harmful because they imply that knowledge is lacking until one reads a book when really truth exists within ones self and one's own reason all along.

It has been asked whether God is personal or impersonal. The absolute supreme God is very personal to the person who has the experience of God. God only seems impersonal to those who have never experienced God. But to those who have experienced God, God is personal. The absolute God and the personal God are identical.

The obtaining of this state is deeply based on morality. Not morality according to other people but morality based on reason, compassion, and love. One must be true to oneself despite what anyone thinks, says, or does. It is achieved through great discipline and an unbreakable faith in reason and true morality. True morality is acting and thinking according to ones reason and being true to one's self. Abelard was correct when he wrote that intentions are more important in morality than actions. People can do seemingly charitable actions for selfish reasons which make the actions immoral. The individual must use his or her own reason to come to enlightenment, it must make sense solely and completely to the individual to be true enlightenment. This is why there are so many religions which are interpretations of the same thing. People used the same reason differently to come to enlightenment, Nirvana, Brahman, the Tao, Allah, God, and Yahweh. Differences in these religions are due to historical and cultural differences in the places and periods which they originated.

Believing and thinking that God exists is not required to be happy. What is required to be happy is being a good person. Atheists can live a happy life and a good life. The experience which is sometimes associated with God is revealed to very few exceptional individuals who experience the beatific vision of the spiritual experience. If someone never experiences this in the person's life it is alright because everyone is always in the state throughout his or her life. Ignorance is a lack of knowledge but just because one is ignorant does not mean the truth is not there. They just don't know they are in the state because they have not realized it within themselves. If a person never has the experience they will be alright because the Good is always present with them and they can still be good and happy. Mystics perceive everything as a universal. God is in all things and God is everywhere which means that God is already in every state of mind and every thing. Thus one is already experiencing the universal of God in everything one is and does. Buddhism provides an atheistic interpretation of the mystical experience calling it Nirvana.

It is said that ignorance is bliss. Knowledge of worldly suffering without divine knowledge leads to sadness. Divine knowledge gives happiness even with knowledge of worldly suffering. In cases of happiness without divine knowledge in which people are ignorant of worldly suffering, they are happy but the happiness is temporal and the state of happiness is subject to misery and sadness. In the state of blissful ignorance people are not really happy if they do not act virtuously in accordance with their essence which is Ultimate Sacred Reality.

The fact that everyone dies is proof that God loves everyone. We are brought into this wondrous existence for a short time and then pass away back to our source and origin which is nothingness. Living forever would eventually be boring, meaningless, and valueless. By living forever one would do the same things over and over again making them meaningless. The mystic would already have attained the purpose of existence making his corporeal life meaningless. We inevitably return to our source which is the purpose of life, to realize our essence. One should not commit suicide but live this wondrous existence for the short time it is one's life. One should realize one's nature which means live a good life and then return to one's source.

Many issues in metaphysics have been discussed in this work. Many of these issues I think are solvable and indeed have been solved. Kant claims that metaphysics as a science is impossible because we have no access to supersensible reality (Copleston 304). Kant is right in a sense. I am doing metaphysics based on my observations, reasoning, and experience. Kant is wrong in claiming we have no intellectual intuitions of things in themselves or of supersensible reality. Many examples have been discussed in this work of people who had intellectual intuitions of supersensible reality. Kant is right in that we only know what we can reason and experience. If someone has an experience of supersensible reality then someone knows something about that reality. It is impossible for the person to prove to others that this experience exists. Schopenhauer is right in that the subject of the experience cannot convince as there is no proof of his experience but the philosopher (Kant in this case) is able to convince. The lack of proof does not make the subject of the experience wrong but it does make his claims unconvincing to others. As has been seen throughout history, just because something is convincing to many people does not make the thing true. Therefore metaphysics based on one's reasoning and experience (as people do have experiences of supersensible reality however do not have philosophical proof of these subjective experiences) is possible as a subject of study. The question may be asked if there is no philosophical proof of these subjective experiences, how can we study them or even know they exist. An individual who has not had the experience does not know for certain that it does exist until the individual has the experience. The experience is attained through wisdom by the method of being wise described in an above section of this essay. We can study the experience through many accounts of people having the experience throughout history. There are too many accounts of people throughout history who did not know anything about each other and describe having very similar mystical experiences for the similarity of the experiences to be a coincidence. For example, the Hindu sages did not know about the Christian mystics and both groups of people describe having a very similar experience. The more one studies these accounts the more one realizes they cannot be coincidences. The study of very similar accounts of individual's subjective experiences of supersensible reality is possible. Therefore in Kant's term of metaphysics as a study of supersensible reality, metaphysics as a subject of study is possible. Kant and I are in agreement in that the arguments proposed to prove the existence of God such as the ontological, cosmological, and teleological arguments are all invalid. These arguments provide evidence but not proof for the existence of God. Taking Kant's Practical Reason into account, Kant and I are in agreement. According to Kant, one attains some knowledge of supersensible reality through morality (Copleston 342-343). As written above one attains metaphysical knowledge through morality. Most of the individuals throughout history gained their metaphysical knowledge through morality and living the good life.

Metaphysics is possible as a subject of study. It is also closely connected to other subjects of philosophy such as Ethics and philosophy of religion. Philosophy of Mind is also closely connected to studying the experience described in this essay. The experience can be studied as psychological but the experience goes beyond Psychology into Metaphysics. Through such experiences metaphysics is intimately connected with the Philosophy of Mind. We can only understand metaphysical entities through our minds. Metaphysical experiences such as altered states of consciousness are very rare and when one has an experience one apprehends the Good, the Beautiful, the True, and Love which a person comprehends as one and the same thing. One attains such an experience through morality, aesthetic contemplation, and great discipline. Such experiences are very difficult to achieve. We cannot know the thing in itself through ordinary conscious experience, but through altered states of consciousness we will be able to grasp what reality truly is.

Wealth can be accumulated in a person's life but the person should still be a good person. One must be unattached and unbonded to one's wealth in order to attain the mystical experience. One must be willing to give up one's wealth at any moment to continue to be in the enlightened state.

One must be good and moral in order to attain and understand metaphysical truths described in the essay above. These metaphysical claims made by individuals may become religious in cases such as Plotinus who had a major influence on Christian and Islamic philosophers (Hyman 5. 217). Religion can be philosophical, but philosophy does not have to be religious. Through philosophy people may realize how to lead the good life of wisdom and may comprehend truths about existence and life.

The essence of Mysticism is in the experience of Ultimate Sacred Reality. This experience is attained through asceticism with the intentions of doing the good and completely eliminating egoism and selfhood. Mystical experience is very difficult to attain. When it is attained it provides an insight into true reality and the meaning of existence. The whole of my philosophy is that through right living and the realization of one's essence one attains spiritual understanding of everything, happiness, peace, and satisfaction.

A Circle as a representation of Mystical Philosophy

A circle represents the structure of the mind and universe with God as a dot in the center. God creates the universe emanating from the center Intelligence which further emanates Matter. The mind lives in a material body and can contemplate the Intelligence and God.

The circle can also represent the mind in its gradations from the thought of matter, abstractions and associations of the mind, and spiritual contemplation to contemplations of God. Our minds can wander all around the circle in associations of ideas.

Appendix

My Personal Mystical Experience

I have attained the spiritual experience. In 2006 I went to a leadership conference in Florida, Fort Lauderdale at Nova southeastern University. The head of the conference gave an opening lecture in which the lecturer talked about a ninety year old woman who said her retirement home room was perfect and needed no change. When asked why she thought this way by someone she said I'm ninety and will not be bothered by imperfections anymore, all is perfect. The head of the conference also talked about Gandhi and told us Gandhi once said don't wish the change, be the change you want to see in the world. We should be the change we want to see in the world. These words inspired me to be a good person. I also wanted to get my money's worth going to the leadership conference. I was also encouraged to be social by my parents. They wanted me to be social at the conference which encouraged me to talk to the other teenagers at the conference. I remember on my way to the conference from Reno leaving my mother at airport security. When my mother and I left each other I looked back at her after I took a few steps and saw her walking in the opposite direction. I felt a sense of loneliness and was a little nervous and frightened traveling for the first time. I did not know then that I would come back a completely different person. Being social at the conference I made new friends quickly. In the cafeteria I noticed all the people in my group were sitting together but I was usually an independent individual and did not want to sit with them just because they were sitting together, so I sat at another table for a few moments but then sat with them since it was boring and awkward sitting alone when they were right there and I could sit with them. We conversed and it was nice. In the conference spending so much time together we quickly became close friends. We talked so much that at the conference I quickly learned how futile being social and talking with people usually is. This caused me to withdraw from being social and external things and turn to an inner peace in myself. Upon doing this people were more distant towards me since I was not conforming to their social group. But I grew in popularity at the conference by being different and still being somewhat social. I probably appeared good looking to them which contributed to my popularity. I must have seemed interesting to them. Once a group called me over to their group in the cafeteria. I think they expected petty behavior from me but I went over to their group, stood tall and asked them what they wanted. I can't remember what they said but I was polite and pleasant towards them. One night at the conference there was a dance. At the dance there was no real dancing but teenagers would rub against one another such as a woman's butt would rub against a man's penis. At the dance I realized the futility of sexual pleasures. The dry humping was pleasurable to my body but not pleasing to my mind. The dry humping seemed as though it was not worth the bodily pleasure attained by doing it. It was not directed toward what is good by the intelligent mind and gave rise to nervousness, degraded behavior which was not conducive to real happiness and virtue. The dry humping caused in me a feeling of anxiety that this activity was not for the good and would result in more pain and less happiness than it seemed to result in. After realizing this I left the dance and walked back to my room. I noticed while walking back that some people were following me. I think they thought I was cool and interesting from my strange behavior. During one night we were waiting for a lecturer to show up who was very late. Waiting in the lecture room I stood up straight in my chair and waited for him. Throughout all this time I constantly directed my mind so that I had complete control over what I was thinking. Whenever an uncontrolled thought entered me I would stop the thought and control it. I controlled my body and mind and did not submit to pleasure or pain and completely controlled my mind. I was waiting for a long time and felt pain in my back and body but did not try to submit to it by relaxing my body. Doing this the people around me did petty things to provoke me and make me feel bad but I kept doing what I was doing with a steadfast Mind doing what I was doing. I felt I could do this all day, perhaps even forever. I felt that way a lot during the conference. In anything we were doing I felt that I could do it all day or forever, in this way every activity was an end in itself and not a means for something else, so I was always complete and fulfilled no matter what I was doing. Sitting as I was in the room waiting for the lecturer I had overcome all bad feelings of being abandoned by my friends and people. I was happy to be so self sufficient. During the conference I walked straight and stood up straight and sat down with a straight back. My posture strengthened my body. Eventually the lecturer arrived and spoke to the people at the conference. He mentioned that most people in the world are very poor and we should do things to improve the world. We should improve the world by improving the places around us. We should improve the world by being courteous to the people around us. People looked at me and perhaps thought I resembled some of the characteristics the lecturer was describing. I thought it is bad that people will characterize me with what the lecturer was saying which happened by chance. After that people seemed to admire me. I talked to one person there who was angry about a fight he got into with his girlfriend. I told him to calm down and get rid of some of his energy by running. He said he does have a lot of energy right now. We ran some across the campus. I said in a short time none of this conference will matter. He said your right. I told him I tried to be social with people but then looked within myself and what I really felt and knew that people were being shallow and insincere. Waiting for the lecturer this friend sat near me and was the only one who sat near me. I gave him a look which may have signified that he shouldn't do that and he did not sit there anymore. Another popular teenager at the conference seemed to admire me. I seemed to get my message across of serenity and goodness to them once without talking and I saw him smile. It was good. When returning to the building we were staying in I spoke to some people outside. Someone suggested he should hit his girlfriend and I said that doesn't solve anything. A girl looked like she was thinking about what I had said. I noticed people in the conference were always looking to find amusement in certain places. They would quickly walk looking for fun and amusement. I realized their search for amusement was futile and they were looking for amusement where no amusement would be found. When the conference was over on the last day a girl was interacting with me. She wanted to be around me it seemed. She said when I was about to leave her you don't smile you don't frown you don't do anything what do you feel. I looked at her and smiled and did not say anything. She smiled and laughed a little. I think I serenely and silently answered her question. I was happy in what I had learned at the conference. One of the counselors on the bus to the airport thanked me and said it was really great having me on the conference. When we got to the airport I was walking toward the wrong place from where I wanted to go. The counselor noticed this and directed me in the right direction. The other people who were at the conference saw this and quickly walked away from me. I think I seemed very god like to them at the conference and since I made this error in front of them they seemed to want to avoid it. I realized from that event that I can make mistakes. I felt good and without pride that I could make mistakes and was not important. Throughout the conference I came to accept that some people were better than me at doing certain things that I wanted to be good at doing. I accepted it serenely and peacefully without pride and without anxiety. This made me able to clear my mind of all feelings of envy and anger. This made me serene and humble. I thought of how some people got better grades than me in school and I thought to myself OK. At the airport I had to wait a long time for my flight to take off. The plane did not leave when it was scheduled to and the airlines were extremely inefficient. The airline people made us move to the terminal right next to the first terminal and then back to the first terminal. The plane was very late in getting to Denver. The whole trip took 12 hours. The plane during the trip stopped at three airports on the way. During all of this I was being pettily harassed by the people on the plane. Despite all of this I remained peaceful and did not get angry. At Denver I had missed my flight and had to wait on a very long and extremely slow line. After waiting for a very long time I began to cry in front of every one. I sat down on the floor and opened my bag and I saw that there was an apple in my bag I could have eaten. I was very hungry and it made me sadder seeing that I could have eaten earlier. I saw everyone noticing me and a security guard was watching me. Some people smiled a little not because I was suffering but because despite this awful situation, I was letting out my frustration by crying and not in a worse way. One of the employees noticed me and said if they new I was 15 they would have moved me up the line quicker. She gave me a place to stay at the airport with other people. The next day I was instructed which terminal I should go to get to Reno. I went to the terminal and while I was waiting I listened to my Ipod. People would pettily get close to me and then go somewhere else. Perhaps I looked different to them than every one else looked. When I got on the plane the flight attendant announced something about an Ipod most likely referring to me. I kept calm throughout the flight with minor petty behavior from the other people on the plane. When I arrived at the Reno airport a little ways into the airport I saw my mom and dad. I had come back to them a completely different person. I was happy to see them and made a loud laugh when I saw them. I was more social, polite, and happier towards them and I really was. My mom said my new behavior was because I was tired but it was because of what I learned at the conference and the airport experience. At the conference I realized what I was going to do for the rest of my life which was develop my education. Most of the teenagers at the conference had no idea what they were going to do for the rest of their lives I thought. A lot of the behavior from some of the other teenagers was petty and ridiculous. The excitement of merely being in the conference at Florida contributed to my mind being developed into excitement and strength as well as toward enlightenment. My mom and dad realized that I was not changing my behavior and my behavior was so strange compared to normal human behavior. I was nice and polite but the way I was those things was strange to them. Eventually my birthday came and I was turning sixteen. My best friend called and I invited him over for my birthday. I tried to teach him what I had learned which was a lot to learn in one day. The things I told him were he should get an education while he can and the opportunity is not available to many people in the world. I told him no one can give you an education, you have to learn on your own. Gaining enlightenment is something a person must do on their own. No one can make you attain it but one must attain it on one's own. My friend must have been shocked by my behavior and how I changed and that was the end of our friendship. The people around me were very petty doing little things to annoy me most likely because of my behavior. I took frequent walks around my neighborhood and I noticed that nature was so beautiful. Nature was more beautiful than it usually looked. During these walks I was experiencing extreme emotional uplifting feelings. It was as if I was at a higher state of reality and I was seeing more clearly. During one of the walks this higher state of reality had risen so high that I experienced an ultimate light of complete bliss and love. Just before I experienced the light I asked how and why were things created and this extreme upsurge of a light that was filled with beauty and love and was beauty and love came out of nowhere and nothing. It was the most amazing thing I had ever experienced. The creation of existence and the meaning of life had been revealed to me. I was supremely happy and supremely joyful. I asked myself if you were to die right now would you be satisfied. I told myself during this period yes. If you are not satisfied to die at the present moment you want something, something is lacking in you which you feel needs to be fulfilled in your life. In the state of enlightenment nothing needs to be done and one is always satisfied and fulfilled. At the conference my mind and thoughts directed me to a feeling of great happiness. I was in the realm of the intelligence which Plotinus wrote about because of my ethical thoughts and ethical behavior. At the conference I tried to eat as healthily as possible. I ate ham and meat but not very much of it and I never drank soft drinks. This contributed to my spiritual experience because it cleansed the body of all unnecessary and unhealthy aspects. But one cannot stay in this supreme experience for long. One must come out of it because one is attached to a body. After the experience I knew my purpose in life is complete. There was nothing left to do. I did not know what else to do so I just did nothing around the house. Eventually the people around me caused me to go back to my ordinary way of life. But I was forever a new person because of what had been revealed to me. During this period I was also obsessed with a girl which contributed negatively psychologically. Something was also trying to intimidate me by making loud booming noises around me which also contributed negatively psychologically. Because of these bad contributions my mind wandered and I obsessed about them. At night in my house I could not go to sleep the whole night I was so excited. Laying in bed at the conference I could not go to sleep because I had not eaten anything before bed to cause me to sleep. I also had not masturbated for a few days during the conference. This activity contributed to me having the spiritual experience. It's as if God loves you so much because of your thoughts and behavior that it gives you enlightened feelings. This is similar to the saying God bless you. From thinking and doing what is good I received this blessedness which is the grace of God. My roommate was somewhat petty in playing with my things while I was in the bathroom and whispering to me incoherent statements when we were trying to sleep. I didn't let it bother me. At the conference from observing the people from different places I learned that people are the same everywhere. But I know the state of consciousness is authentic. It was the best and greatest thing that ever happened to me.

Descriptions of Philosophers, Mystics, and Terms in the Mystical Tradition

There are many examples of individual people who have experienced Ultimate Sacred Reality which is another term for God. These mystics represent some of the world's religious traditions as well as some of the world's philosophical traditions. How they express mystical views shall be described next. Many of these philosophies are different expressions and interpretations of the same thing which is the greatest spiritual experience. There are others with very similar ideas which were not included on this list. One should not reject philosophies that arise in the future that are similar to the ones such as Platonism and Buddhism. Just because they call the same things by different names does not make their ideas different. There will most likely always be a few and very rare exceptional individuals who have the spiritual experience. The mystics claim that through this spiritual experience they have realized the goal and purpose of life which is the experience of and the union with ultimate sacred reality.

This list is not exhaustive and there are many other individuals who have achieved the same mystical state not mentioned here. These figures and synonymous concepts manifest all throughout history.

In Chinese Philosophy, Tai ji is the great ultimate. This great ultimate is similar to the concept of God. All things come from Tai ji and flow back to Tai ji. All things are in constant flux except for Tai ji. In the philosophy of Heraclitus everything is in constant flux except for the logos which is an eternal divine reason and is also similar to Tai ji.

Taoist sages describe mystical experiences. Lao Tse (6th-4th centuries BCE) -Ancient Chinese sage who may have been an imaginary figure who is considered to have written the Tao Te Ching. The Tao te Ching describes many moral practices such as patience, compassion, and simplicity as essential to living a good life. The book also describes the Tao which is the way of all things. The Tao cannot be expressed adequately in language and is beyond language. The Tao is described as the ultimate reality. Lao tse describes the Tao as the source of everything including the spiritual experience. Chuang tze was an ancient daoist sage who thought that the spiritual experience was becoming one with and knowing nature. The spiritual experience is as if a person is at one with nature. Spinoza thought knowing God was the same thing as knowing nature. The daoist sages such as Chuang tse and the writers of the Tao te Ching describe knowing the Dao which is the eternal way.

Hermes Trismegistus was an Egyptian prophet, sage, and holy man. He thought the mind of some men who possess intellect can attain divine experience with God. He thought men should detach themselves from their corporeal bodies by contemplating higher things such as God through the intellect. He had an influence on subsequent philosophers, especially Platonists.

Confucius (551-479 BCE)- Ancient Chinese sage who wrote about propriety and proper rules of conduct which are necessary in order to rule a state well. Many of the rules of conduct Confucius describes are important in order to attain the spiritual experience. Confucius writes about the virtuous conduct of the superior man who is the wise man.

The Bhagavad Gita is an ancient Hindu sacred scripture which describes virtuous and godlike behavior in the sense of being free from the passions and from desire as well as transcending pleasure and pain. According to the Bhagavad Gita, he who conquers his passions conquers all things and becomes one with Brahman.

Siddartha Gautama (563-480 BCE) became the Buddha who was a spiritual teacher and the founder of Buddhism. He claimed to have attained enlightenment and nirvana and lived an ascetic life.

Nirvana and enlightenment are mystical because they are terms for a spiritual experience which is often described as ineffable.

Parmenides (born 515 BCE) was a Pre Socratic Greek philosopher who thought that the One exists and the Many which is the world of plurality does not exist. The material and sensual world of plurality is an illusion. This is very similar to the Hindu concept of Maya which is illusion. According to Parmenides' teacher Xenophanes the One and God are identical. Ascending to the One is the same thing as ascending to God which leads to union with God and the One.

Pythagoras (570-495 BCE) Pre Socratic philosopher, in the Golden verses of Pythagoras the good life is described as being chaste, controlling ones passions, and living intelligently with discipline. By living the good life the Golden Verses of Pythagoras conclude that a person will be a God. The person will be a God in the sense of not being disturbed by human problems. The person will be a God in the sense of being indifferent to pain and pleasure. The person will be liberated from all conflict. Being a God is being the wise man. Empedocles also supported some ascetic tendencies such as abstaining from meat. He stated that all has been liberated in the attainment of the God head.

Plato (428-348 BCE)- Greek Philosopher who developed a metaphysical system which claimed that there is a higher reality and true reality consisting of Ideas. These ideas are what is truly real and sensual things and material things are imitations of these Ideas which are the higher reality and the true reality. The highest and greatest Idea is the Idea of the Good. The Idea of the Good is the same thing as the one of Plotinus and God. Plato uses metaphorical language to describe a person's mental ascent to this higher reality. For example in the Phaedrus Plato writes about a chariot ascending to the heavens which is a metaphor for a person's mind ascending to a higher state of consciousness in which the person knows the Ideas and the Idea of the Good. The Idea of the Good is expressed as the Beautiful in the dialogue the Symposium. In the Symposium Socrates describes a persons union with the Beautiful. In the allegory of the cave an individual comes out of the cave which represents the material world of ignorance. The individual comes out of the cave and sees the sun which represents the Idea of the Good.

Aristotle (384-322 BCE) Greek Philosopher who writes about the experience as being in God's contemplative state. According to Aristotle humans can attain a state of perfect contemplation which is the state that God is in all the time. This state of perfect contemplation is very similar to union with God. Aristotle realizes that human beings cannot be in God's state of perfect contemplation all the time. For Aristotle the greatest activity is contemplation. God is always in a state of perfect contemplation and humans sometimes achieve God's state. Aristotle wrote about the soul which is another term for the mind. According to Aristotle, there is within the soul the passive intellect and the active intellect. The passive intellect takes in information and processes it to become actual knowledge. The active intellect is actual knowledge. When a person realizes his or her active intellect Aristotle claims the person sees all things. Some philosophers have claimed that the active intellect is identical with God and is the part of the soul which is immortal. When a person actualizes his or her active intellect the person attains the state of perfect contemplation which is the state of God.

Aristotle thinks the only substances or Forms that are separate from material things are God, the intelligences of the Spheres, and the active intellect (Copleston 306). Aristotle thought that some Forms were immaterial (Copleston 306). Plato and Aristotle agreed in that they both thought there were some immaterial Forms. There is a resemblance in Aristotelian philosophy, Platonism, and Neo-Platonism because all philosophies contain a hierarchy of being. God, the Form of the Good, and the One are the highest. Spherical intelligences, immaterial Forms, and the intelligence are the second highest being. And the active intellect, the rational soul, and the soul are the lowest. All these philosophers thought that some entities are immaterial. All of these philosophies are similar in that they all contain a similar hierarchy of being.

Epicurus (341- 270 BCE)- Greek philosopher and the founder of Epicureanism. He thought that pleasure which resulted from having no desires and peace of mind is good. Epicurus also thought people should not fear death. He thought prudence is an essential virtue. The pleasant life and the virtuous life are identical. A person is able to become a God in the sense of being liberated from all worldly problems and temptations. Being a God results from virtuous conduct and being wise. The mystic embodies the divine in the world in the sense of becoming wise.

Stoicism was an ancient philosophical school and the three tenets of Stoicism are materialism, mutation, and monism. All things are material, all things constantly change, and all things are ultimately one which is a materialistic and pantheistic God. A person should not let external things which are outside the person's control affect him or her. A person should live moderately and without desire. A person should conform to his or her own nature which is the natural order of all things. By living according to Stoic precepts one will know nature and be happy. Many of the stoic precepts are characteristics of the mystic and wise man. The stoics were right when they wrote that the only thing one should do is conform to one's own nature. This means one should realize one's essence within which means be good, virtuous, and attain the spiritual experience. One should act in accordance to Nature. One should let events happen as they naturally occur and realize an individual cannot control most things that happen in Nature. Nature is the only true harmony. The most peaceful life is the best life. To wish for something that depends on others can enslave. It is better that the Intellect controls the emotions. Discern what can be controlled and what cannot. Do not give your mind over to confusion. The divine order of nature should be our goal.

Marcus Aurelius (121-180)- Roman Emperor and philosopher who wrote that a person should be kind, honest, polite, compassionate, and intelligent to other people. Marcus Aurelius also thought that a person should act and conform with one's own nature. Acting in accordance with one's nature is being what one truly is which is being in accordance with nature. Many of the rules of conduct which Aurelius expresses are aspects of the mystic.

Philo of Alexandria (20 BCE-50 CE) Jewish Philosopher who thought that God does not directly interact with the world. The logos is a mediation between God and the world. The world and God only interact through the logos. This is very similar to the divine will in Ibn Gabirol's philosophy. It is also very similar to Platonism as representing a hierarchy of being. Philo tried to reconcile religion such as Judaism with philosophy such as Platonism. He also thought it is possible to attain mystical union with God.

Plotinus (204-270)- Neo Platonic Philosopher. The term Neo-Platonism was invented in the nineteenth century. Plotinus was a mystic and Platonist. He thought that all creation emanates from the One. It is the purpose of all humans to attain union with the One. Plotinus describes God as the One which is a unity of everything. Plotinus tried to unify different philosophical systems into one system which culminated in Plotinus' philosophy. Neo-Platonism is a unique example of a non religious mystical philosophy.

Origen (184-253)- Christian philosopher in the patristic period who thought a person can attain union with God. Origen also thought that in the end everyone will be saved. A person ascends to God through the trinity. The Holy Ghost signifies higher states of consciousness but not the highest state of consciousness which is God. And the father represents the highest state of consciousness which is God. The doctrine of the trinity consists of the father, the son, and the holy spirit. It is written that the trinity is both three and one. The trinity is both three and one because the same divinity is expressed in three different ways. The father God is expressed through the son which is Jesus Christ through the power of divine grace which is the holy spirit. The holy spirit is the mediation through which knowledge of God is attained. The holy spirit is God because they are made of the same divine force which is love, beauty, and grace and the holy spirit is fully expressed through Jesus Christ. According to one of my professors the three entities of the trinity parallel the three primal hypostases of Neo-Platonism. The father, holy spirit, and son parallel the One, the intelligence, and the soul of Neo-Platonism in that they are the same thing.

Gnosticism was a Christian movement in the Patristic period. The Gnostics were a sect of

Christianity considered heretical by the Orthodox Church. Gnosticism is similar to Neo Platonism in that Gnostics describe the ascent to God. They thought that there is a perfect God and a demiurge. The imperfect and evil demiurge created the universe which is imperfect and evil. The Gnostics thought that all matter is evil. Matter is evil because it is vulnerable to loss. One could easily lose a limb and be disabled for the rest of one's life. One who does not acquire food which is made up of matter will go hungry and may starve. Matter is evil and according to the Gnostics most people are made up of matter and entirely subject to evil. There are a few who contain spirit within them who are able to acquire knowledge of the perfect spirit which will liberate these souls from the world of matter. The Gnostics too thought it is possible to attain union with God which is the supreme spirit and is liberating to the individual who acquires this divine knowledge.

Enactites were an ascetic sect of Christianity during the patristic period who were against marriage, in favor of chastity, against eating meat and were called the water drinkers. All of these ascetic qualities are conducive towards divine experience.

Nagarjuna (ca 150-250)- Mahayana Buddhist philosopher who described the limits of language in trying to describe enlightenment and Nirvana. His writings contradict one another but the contradictions are meant to show that enlightenment and nirvana are beyond the ability to be described by language. Nagarjuna claims that the spiritual experience is beyond language. The Buddha was sometimes silent about some questions asked by his disciples. The silence is meant to indicate that the answers to the questions about nirvana, enlightenment, and emptiness and nothingness cannot be answered using language. One must contemplate in silence to gain the answers to all things. The questions can only be answered by the spiritual experience which is enlightenment.

St. Augustine (354-430 CE) Christian Philosopher and Theologian. St. Augustine was influenced by Plato. He also thought that the soul can attain union with God. Augustine presents a theory of Illuminationism in which one can attain knowledge of the divine ideas that are in God. This is similar to the Ideas of Plato and the intelligences of Neo-Platonism.

Boethius (477-524)- Roman Philosopher who also writes about the experience of the supreme good which is God. Happiness is the attainment of God. The good people and the virtuous people are the people who are truly and really happy and the wicked are miserable. The universe is the best universe which is governed by God. Any person who is virtuous and good will become a God in the sense of experiencing union with God and will be indifferent to pleasure and pain. A person will not be disturbed by any evil that happens to one. These accounts are very similar to doctrines in mysticism.

Pseudo Dionysius (5th-6th centuries CE)- Christian Theologian and mystic who wrote about the union with God. Pseudo Dionysius also writes about the darkness above the light which is a state of the mind above union with God in which there is nothingness which is the ground God is from. God is dependent on nothing and God came out of nothing. It is a state of complete nonattachment. There is absolutely no bondage to anything in the state of nothingness. All things come from God which comes from nothingness which means all things come from nothingness. In this state of nothingness which is another expression for ultimate sacred reality, there is no distinction between the sacred and the profane which are synonymous to samsara and nirvana. At this highest state of consciousness it is realized that All is One and One is All and there is absolutely no distinction between the secular and the sacred. In the state of nothingness one realizes that God is always present in everything whether one knows about it or not.

John Scotus Eriugena (800-877)- Philosopher who synthesized Neo-Platonism and Christianity. He claimed that the final purpose of everything is to attain God. A person can attain and experience God. God created the world through emanations of itself. God is both the efficient and final cause of everything. The efficient cause is the source of an effect, the final cause is the purpose and goal of a thing. All things are directed to God and all things come from God. God is the goal of all things and people have the ability to know God. In a sense all things are already with God but the things do not know and realize that they are with God. Just because someone does not know about something does not mean the unknown thing does not exist. Ignorance also does not mean the unknown thing is not with someone, it just means the unknown thing is not realized in the mind.

Al Farabi (872-950)- Muslim Philosopher who thought that Allah emanates spherical intelligences and the sub lunar realm of the world is the lowest realm of these emanations which means the sub lunar realm is the furthest realm from Allah. This means Allah's presence is least noticeable in the sub lunar realm. The sub lunar realm is the realm of sensual experience and thus the realm furthest removed from Allah. Al Farabi also thought it is possible for a person to gain supreme happiness and knowledge of Allah which is God.

Ibn Sina (980 1037)- Muslim Philosopher who also thought it was possible for a person to attain union with Allah. He has a similar theory of emanation from Allah like Al Farabi's theory.

Al Ghazali (1058-1111)- Muslim Sufi (mystic) who also wrote about the union with Allah and divine intoxication. Al Arabi (1165-1240) was another Islamic mystic.

Al Hallaj (858-922)- A mystic who was executed for exclaiming "I am the Truth" after his mystical experience. The union of his mind with the mind of Allah resulted in what he said.

Jallal udin Rumi (1207-1273)- Persian poet who wrote there are many roads which lead to the same goal, namely union with God. There are many ways to attain the spiritual experience and many interpretations of the way to attain the spiritual experience and expressions of the experience itself. All of the world religions describe different expressions of attaining the experience of ultimate sacred reality. The different expressions of different religions and philosophies are the many roads which lead to union with God which is the experience of ultimate sacred reality.

Ibn Gabirol (1021-1070)- Jewish Neo-Platonist who thought the world emanates from God. There is a mediation between the world and God which is the Divine will. God does not interact with the world directly but only indirectly through the divine will. Ibn Gabirol also thought that union with God and supreme happiness is the highest purpose of human kind.

Saadia Gaon (882-942)- Jewish Thinker who also thought it is possible for the mind to attain God.

Maimonides (1138-1204)- Jewish philosopher who thought that the purpose of all the Jewish writings including the Talmud, Torah, and Mishnah is to perfect the mind and body. When the mind and body are perfected one will attain union with God. Maimonides thought that the prophet and holy person will not indulge in pleasures which is part of the perfection of the mind and body. Maimonides also thought that if religious scriptures are properly interpreted which requires metaphorical interpretation sometimes, they agree with philosophical truths. Philosophy and Religion are compatible.

Kabbalah is Jewish mysticism. In Kabbalah there is a hierarchy of being with ein sof translated as limitless and infinite as the highest and greatest being which is God. Below ein sof are the sefirot which are the ideas of God. These include beauty, power, love, perfection, and wisdom. It is the duty of people to attain towards the sefirot which enables them to attain unification with God and perfection.

Christian von Rosenroth (1636-1689)- Christian Author who wrote the Kabbalah Denudatta. This book was an attempt to explain Kabbalah to Christians. Rosenroth thought Kabbalah was in agreement with Christianity and tried to convert Jews based on the agreement. He thought in the end every person would be saved. He also agreed with the Kabbalist Isaac Luria who thought evil was due to God transcending himself which resulted in left over material which became evil. It is the duty of people to overcome evil and they will eventually do so. Luria and Rosenroth both thought all people would be saved. Saved means become good people and attain union with God. In a sense the idea that everyone will be saved is true in that everyone will die and in death we become nothingness again which is similar to the nothingness of the highest state of consciousness. In death one will not be conscious of anything but one will be nothingness.

Shankara (788-820)- Hindu Philosopher and the main advocate of the Advaita Vedanta Philosophy. According to this philosophy the supreme truth of everything is Brahman and Brahman is ultimately one. There is no duality and the sensual universe is an illusion. The illusion is called Maya. The self which is atman is ultimately identical with Brahman. Shankara emphasized having no desires and desires are hindrances to the self achieving union with Brahman. Brahman is the true reality and the minds lower states of consciousness outside of Brahman are illusions. The mind is always with Brahman and the states of the mind outside of Brahman are illusory.

Ramanuja (1017- 1137)- Hindu Philosopher who responded to the teachings of Shankara. Ramanuja criticized the teaching of Shankara which claimed that nirguna Brahman (ultimate, absolute, Brahman with no attributes) cannot exist without attributes. According to Ramanuja everything that exists has an attribute. According to Shankara, nirguna Brahman has no attributes. Some claim that nirguna Brahman cannot be adequately expressed in words. Ramanuja wants to express nirguna Brahma by describing nirguna Brahman. In order to describe what transcends language Ramanuja wants to ascribe attributes to nirguna Brahman. Ramanuja realizes that the linguistic description of the experience of Brahman is not the same thing as the experience itself. Ramanuja wants to describe nirguna Brahman and in order to do that Ramanuja must describe what nirguna Brahman is like and Ramanuja uses attributes to do that. Ramanuja claims that if a person lives a life that is pleasing to Brahman the person will attain supreme bliss of Brahman's nature which is the spiritual experience.

Madhva (1238-1317)- Hindu Philosopher who criticized the Advaita Vedanta Philosophy claiming that it contradicts sensual experience. The Advaita Vedanta philosophy refers to experience as illusion and does not deny it exists. Sensual experience exists but it is an illusion and is not true reality. The true reality which is Brahman transcends sensual experience and reveals that sensual experience is illusory.

Hugh of St. Victor (1096-1141)- German Philosopher at the school of St. Victor who spoke of a person's divine contemplation of God and knowing God.

Bonaventure (1221-1274)- Christian Theologian and Philosopher who described the union of the mind and God. He also proposed a theory of exemplarism which is similar to Augustine's theory of illuminationism. According to the theory in the mind of God there are divine ideas. Knowledge of these ideas is possible.

Thomas Aquinas (1225-1274)- Christian Theologian and Philosopher who claimed that the greatest happiness is for the mind to attain God. The goal and purpose of all human life is to attain the beatific vision which is union with God. Humans achieve this state through virtue.

Dante (1265-1321)- the author of the Divine Comedy. In the last Canto of Paradiso, Dante describes the state of union with God as ecstasy, bliss, and sublimity.

Meister Eckhart (1260-1328)- Christian Theologian, Neo Platonist, and Mystic. Christian theologian and mystic. Eckhart tried to reconcile Christianity and Neoplatonism. He describes the divine spark of the soul which is the most profound part of the person and is identical with God. A person can realize the divine spark of the soul and attain union with God. The divine spark of the soul is similar to Aristotle's active intellect. When a person realizes the divine spark of the soul which is the active intellect the person is unified with God. When one realizes one's active intellect one attains the perfect contemplation which God has. This is the same thing as the identity of atman and Brahman in Hinduism. The active intellect, the divine spark, and atman are identical with God and Brahman. The inner essence of one's mind is identical with the universal essence of existence. God is within you. Eckhart also wrote that God is present in all things. Eckhart thought the experience of God transcends language.

Thomas a Kempis was a monk and most likely the author of The Imitation of Christ which contains spiritual instructions on how to attain the good and saintly life.

Saint Theresa (1515-1582)- Christian Mystic who wrote about her experiences of union with God. She wrote of the spiritual experience as ecstasy and rapture. Saint Catherine of Siena and Saint Catherine of Genoa also had mystical experiences of God. Mechthild of Magdeburg, Julian of Norwich, and Hildegard of Bingen were Christian mystics who all describe having spiritual experiences. St John of the Cross was a Christian mystic and wrote about union with God. All of these Saints were Mystics of Medieval Times. Ruysbroeck was a Christian mystic in the middle ages who wrote of three unities. There is the unity of the soul in God, there is the unity in the Holy Spirit, and there is the unity in the world of the senses. Ruysbroeck claims that the harmony of these three unities culminates in union with God.

Miguel de Molinos (1628-1696)- Spanish Holy Man who revived Quietism which is a mystical movement which claims silence and quiet calmness can lead to God. Contemplating silence is like contemplating nothingness and can lead to what the Indian Religions call Om which is complete nonattachment, tranquility, and peace as well as sublimity in knowing the emptiness of all things. He tried to find a way toward union with God without intermediaries claiming through the church and through Christ as means one attains union with God as an end. Silesius was a German poet and mystic who thought God and man are essentially one. They are one in their essence which is the essence of the soul. The soul is the mind. Schopenhauer wrote that all of the accounts which these mystics give provide a practical proof regarding the truth of mysticism.

Marsilio Ficino and Pico della Mirandolla were two Italian Neo-Platonists in the fifteenth century. They attempted to reconcile Christianity and Neo-Platonism and thought men could attain mystical experience. They thought different philosophical systems were compatible and tried to unify them under the Platonic philosophy.

Jacob Boehme (1575-1624)- German Mystic who wrote of his experiences of divine light. He wrote of the experience as a unique perception of things such that all things are beautiful and related to God. He wrote about Sophia which is wisdom. He wrote that Sophia leads the person to the divine. Sophia is like a mother and bride who comforts and cherishes a person towards the experience with the divine. Sophia is wisdom and right reason and wisdom leads toward the divine.

John Milton (1608-1674)- English Poet who wrote long and hard is the path out of darkness leading to light. The way to attain union with God which is the light Milton writes about is very difficult. It requires great discipline and a very virtuous character. People are in the darkness which is the lack of knowledge of God and it requires much effort and hard work to attain union with God.

Baruch Spinoza (1632-1677)- Philosopher who proposed a philosophy of pantheistic monism. Spinoza wrote about the intellectual love of God. This love of God enables a person to know God. Spinoza describes the state of knowing God as an excellent and rare state which is also very difficult to achieve. Spinoza claims that God, substance, and Nature are identical. According to Spinoza virtue is right reason and the person who is not controlled by his or her passions is virtuous.

William Law (1686-1761)- English Cleric and Mystic who wrote people should live the divine life which is the ascetic life of love. Jonathan Edwards

(1703-1758)-American Cleric and Theologian. He thought it is possible to experience the divine. All things are in the mind of God.

William Blake (1757-1827)- English Poet who wrote that all religions are one and are expressions of the poetic genius. All religions are expressions of the One which is the ultimate reality. Madame Guyon (1648-1717) was a French mystic who describes accounts she had of the spiritual experience.

Immanuel Kant (1724-1804)- German Philosopher who thought that theoretical knowledge of supersensible reality is impossible, however through morality people can acquire some knowledge of supersensible reality. Most of the people who have attained mystical experience lived lives of disciplined moral conduct. Morality enabled them to attain mystical experience. In many cases people have attained mystical experience through virtue and living lives of strict moral conduct. Kant is correct in claiming that some knowledge of supersensible reality is attained through morality.

Johann Fichte (1762-1814)-German Philosopher who thought the external world is the non ego and a person which is the ego should do moral actions in the external world as a means to self realization. The realization of the self is the goal of a person and one becomes better through moral self realization. Fichte describes morality as a means to attain a goal. Morality is used to attain one's goal as a subject.

Friedrich Schelling (1775-1854)- German Philosopher who wrote about the Absolute. He wrote about the relationship of subject and object. Schelling attempted to synthesize the subject and object and claimed that they were the same thing which he also claimed to be true in regards to Idealism and Realism. Schelling thought beauty and truth are the same thing. He thought union with the Absolute is possible in a sense which is similar to Neo-Platonism.

Georg Hegel (1770-1831)- German Philosopher who developed a philosophy of the Absolute. According to Hegel, the Absolute coming to know itself and a person coming to know the Absolute are the same thing. The Absolute is another term for God. Hegel thought the subject of theology and philosophy is the same which is God, the Absolute, and the Whole. According to Hegel the rational is the real and the real is the rational. Hegel writes that philosophy is concerned with the truth and the truth is the whole.

Arthur Schopenhauer (1788-1860)- German Philosopher who thought existence was in itself evil. Schopenhauer was so disgusted by the evils and misery he observed in the world he thought existence was metaphysically evil. One can temporarily escape the evil of existence through art and aesthetic contemplation. Permanent escape from the evil of existence consisted in complete withdrawal from the world and living an ascetic life. Despite his negative views on the essential nature of all things Schopenhauer concludes that the best life is the ascetic life and writes about many ascetics who achieved union with God which Schopenhauer describes as the negation of existence. Evil, pain, and existence are positive things for Schopenhauer and goodness, pleasure, and nothingness are negations of these things. The ascetic who has denied, withdrawn from, and overcome the evil world is the best and most good person. Complete withdrawal and overcoming the world occurs in the experience which is described as union with God.

Friedrich Nietzsche (1844-1900)- German Philosopher who never described mystical experience in detail but nevertheless wrote about things an individual should do to attain mystical experience. An individual must overcome oneself. In order to do that an individual must make something better of one's self and become a greater individual. Nietzsche wrote about higher individuals who had overcome themselves. Nietzsche was a nonconformist and thought an individual should have great freedom to develop himself into his own magnificence. Nietzsche wrote against mainstream morality because he thought morality was being used to keep higher and greater individuals from being greater individuals. He thought Morality was being used by narrow minded people to further there own interests and the interests of the species. What is considered conducive to the species and what preserves the species is considered moral and what does not is called immoral and evil. Individuals must transcend themselves and make something greater of themselves in order to attain mystical experience. Nietzsche wrote I love him who creates something greater than himself and then perishes. Nietzsche thought one should be who one truly is. In mysticism one truly is one's inner essence which is God.

Carl Jung (1875-1961)- German Psychologist who wrote about accounts of people who claimed to have experiences of knowing God. Jung thought these accounts were true. Jung also thought there was a collective unconscious shared by everyone which is the source of the representations of symbols which occur throughout all humanity. He called these symbols Mandalas. Jung thought that people could attain the spiritual experience of ultimate sacred reality.

John Keats (1795-1821)- English Poet who thought that beauty and truth are the same thing. In the higher state of consciousness beauty and truth are identical. The One is the true, the beautiful, the good, and love. Fractals truly illustrate what Keats called the equivalence of beauty and truth as well as harmony. Through mathematics both beauty and truth are known to be the same.

Soren Kierkegaard (1813-1855) Danish Religious Philosopher who thought that the religious life is the best life and the aesthetic life of pleasure is unfulfilling. The ethical life in which marriage is included is better than the aesthetic life. The ascetic and religious life is considered the best life by Kierkegaard. For Kierkegaard truth is striving towards the objective uncertainty in which a person does not know if God exists. This is faith that there is intrinsic good in existence. Kierkegaard calls the spiritual experience the highest.

Ralph Waldo Emerson (1803-1882)- American Writer who proposed the idea of Transcendentalism. According to Transcendentalism a person should be a nonconformist. A person should be an individual. There is an over soul which is synonymous with the One of Neo-Platonism. The over soul expresses ideas toward a person's individual soul and through this process a person comes to know the over soul. A person should not imitate others but rather should be oneself and come to know the truth through one's own method and way. One may contradict one's self in language if linguistic contradiction is conducive to self development and self improvement.

Main de Biran (1766-1824)- French Philosopher who wrote of the spiritual life of man in which the divine spirit communicates love towards man. Main de Biran claims it is possible for man to be absorbed in God in which God is for man all in all. This means the experience of God is a spiritual experience of everything, in this sense God is all. God as all is in all particular things.

Maurice Blondel (1861-1949)- French Philosopher who maintained that it is possible to attain union with God and live a uniquely religious life. A person chooses to live a religious life or chooses not to. By choosing a life in accordance to God one transcends one's self. One may transcend one's self instead of living a human life engaging in worldly pursuits and pleasures.

Muhammad Iqbaal (1877-1938)- Muslim Philosopher who analyzed Kant's philosophy and concluded it is possible to know the thing in itself because space and time are not fixed entities but are relative to a subject.

This parallels Einstein's theory that they are relative. Iqball concludes that the thing in itself is knowable. The thing in itself is God.

Ramakrishna (1836-1886)- Hindu Mystic who taught that all religions are true and lead to union with God. He also taught that greed, sexual desire, and worldly pursuits were all hindrances to attaining complete spiritual fulfillment in God. Worldly pursuits are ultimately unsatisfying. Ramakrishna claimed to have had mystical experiences of union with Brahma. Ramakrishna is one of many examples of an individual who attained the spiritual experience. He also thought that Islam, Christianity, and Hinduism were all expressions of the same truth.

Martin Heidegger (1889-1976)- German Philosopher who wrote about authenticity and throwness. Throwness is a person accepting what has been given him or her in life without doing what the person really wants to do. Throwness is conformity to how others characterize one and how others expect one to act. In throwness a person's self is not one's own but the person is controlled by how others want the person to be. Authenticity is an individual doing what the individual really wants to do. Authenticity is not conforming and doing what others expect and want one to do. One's self is authentic when one's self is completely one's own and one can make of one's self whatever one wants to make of one's self. An authentic self is conducive in order for one to attain enlightenment and union with God which are different names of the same spiritual experience. One must do it on one's own and not because others expect one to do it.

Jean Paul Sartre (1905-1980) - French Philosopher who distinguished between transcendence and facticity. Transcendence and facticity parallel the authenticity and throwness of Heidegger. Sartre calls bad faith the thought that an individual is unable to realize his or her transcendence. An individual can engage in what Sartre calls transcendence to attain the spiritual experience.

The mystical tradition continued in the Twentieth Century.

Gandhi (1869-1948) - Activist and Ascetic who lived by many ascetic moral sanctions in accordance with spirituality. He thought God is truth and all religions are expressions of the same truth.

Thomas Merton (1915-1968) - Mystic, Writer, and Trappist Monk who wrote about contemplation and the experience of the divine.

John Hick (1922-2012) - Philosopher and Religious Pluralist. A religious pluralist is someone who thinks that all religions are true and are different interpretations of the same thing. Hick wrote about the transcendent and the Real as what transcends sensual reality. The transcendent and the Real are called God in some religious traditions. The mind can attain union with the Real.

Work Cited

Aquinas, Thomas. <u>Selected Writings</u>. Penguin Group. New York. 1998.

Boethius. <u>The Consolation of Philosophy.</u> Penguin Classics. London. 1999.

Capra, Fritjof. <u>The Tao of Physics.</u> Shambhala Publications, Inc. Boston. 1999.

Cheney, Sheldon. <u>Men Who Have Walked With God.</u> Alfered A. Knopf. New York. 1946.

Confucious. <u>The Analects.</u> Dover Publications. New York. 1971.

Copleston, F.C. <u>A History of Philosophy Volumes 1, 4, 6, 7, 8, 9.</u> Doubleday. New York. 1993, 1994.

Copleston, F.C. <u>Religion and the One.</u> Continuum. London. 2002.

D'Olivet, Fabre. Golden Verses of Pythagoras. Noble Offset Printers, Inc. New York. 1975.

Eckhart, edited by Oliver Davies. <u>Selected Writings.</u> Penguin Classics. New York. 1994.

Elwes, R.H.M. <u>Benedict de Spinoza On the improvement of the Understanding, The Ethics, Correspondence.</u> Dover Publications, Inc. New York. 1955.

Eshellman, Andrew. <u>Readings in the Philosophy of Religion.</u> Blackwell Publishing. Oxford. 2008.

Kazin, Alfred. The Portable Blake. Penguin Group. New York. 1974.

Kierkegaard, Soren. Works of Love. Harper Perennial Modern Classics. New York. 2009.

MacKenna, Stephen. Plotinus The Six Enneads. Encyclopedia Britannica, Inc. Chicago.

McKeon, Richard. Reeve, C.D.C. The Basic Works of Aristotle. Random house, Inc. New York. 2001.

Mitchell, Stephen. The Tao te Ching. Harper and Row. New York. 1988.

Nietzsche, Fredrich. The Pre-Platonic Philosophers. Walter Durgreiter. Berlin. 1995.

Popkin, Richard H. The Columbia History of Western Philosophy. Columbia UP. New York. 1999.

Ramakrishna. Wikipedia the Free Encyclopedia. 12-31-11.

Schopenhauer, Arthur. The World as Will and Representation Volume 1 and 2. Dover Publications, Inc. New York. 1969.

Shankara. Wikipedia the Free Encyclopedia. 12-31-11.

Winkworth, Susan (translator). Theologia Germanica. Stuart and Watkins. London. 1966.

Recommended Additional Sources

Churton, Tobias. Gnostic Philosophy. Inner Traditions. Rochester. 2005.

Hick, John. The Fifth Dimension. One World publications. Oxford. 2004.

Huxley, Aldous. The Perennial Philosophy. Perennial. New York. 2004.

Printed in the United States
By Bookmasters